PENGUI
ENGLISH GRAMMAR
EXERCISES

With Answers

James O'Driscoll

ELT

PENGUIN BOOKS

Published by the Penguin Group
27 Wrights Lane, London W8 5TZ, England
Viking Penguin Inc., 40 West 23rd Street, New York, New York 10010, USA
Penguin Books Australia Ltd, Ringwood, Victoria, Australia
Penguin Books Canada Ltd, 2801 John Street, Markham, Ontario, Canada L3R 1B4
Penguin Books (NZ) Ltd, 182–190 Wairau Road, Auckland 10, New Zealand

Penguin Books Ltd, Registered Offices: Harmondsworth, Middlesex, England

First published 1990

Set in Linotron 202 Plantin Roman

Made and printed in Great Britain by
BPCC Hazell Books Ltd
Member of BPCC Ltd
Aylesbury, Bucks, England

CONTENTS

INTRODUCTION

About the book

This is a book of practice on the system of English. It is divided into twenty-five sections. Each section covers an area of basic grammar and contains a number of exercises.

The exercises are not all the same length. Some exercises have only four questions, but others have twenty questions or more. This is because some areas of grammar are more important than others. There is also a section of extra practice at the end of the book. This section helps you with things which are especially difficult.

This book tests your knowledge of English grammar and, more importantly, it gives you practice in using your knowledge to make correct and appropriate sentences. When you do the exercises, you will see that grammar is not just a game. Grammar has meaning – if you change some of the grammar in a sentence, you also change its meaning.

If you want, you can use this book together with *Penguin Basic English Grammar*. Each exercise has a reference to *Penguin Basic English Grammar*. For example, on page 36 you will see: **8.3** The verb **have** (PBEG 25; 40.2). This means that Units 25 and 40.2 of *Penguin Basic English Grammar* have the information you need to do the exercise. But you do not have to use PBEG if you don't want to; perhaps you can do the exercises in this book without it!

Please note that this book is *not* for complete beginners. It is written for elementary students. However, because it emphasises meaning, you may also find it useful if you are at a higher level.

Some advice

It is best to work through a section from beginning to end. This is because the exercises and the questions are in a special order; this order helps you to learn more and makes the differences between things clearer.

Many of the exercises in this book ask you to complete a sentence by putting a word in a gap. In these exercises, it is very important to read the whole sentence carefully. The whole sentence gives you the meaning and the meaning will help you to decide how to fill in the gap.

You should not try to go too fast. With most of the exercises, you will need to think to get the answers right; it may also help you to write your answers down. Please remember that sometimes more than one answer to a question is possible.

NOTE   There are very few grammar words in this book. There is a short list of useful words on the next page to help you understand them.

SOME USEFUL WORDS

AUXILIARY VERB   in the verb formation **have worked, have** is an auxiliary. In **have been working, have** and **been** are auxiliaries. Auxiliary verbs are important for making questions and continuous, perfect and passive verb formations.

CLAUSE   examples of clauses are:
that he has gone in **I know that he has gone;**
when I see him in **I'll tell him when I see him.**

Clauses have subjects and verbs but they cannot make a sentence alone.

FORM   the exact shape of a word. For example, many adverbs end with **-ly** (e.g. **largely**), so we say that many adverbs have a **-ly** form. Some words have only one form. For example, the only form of **the** is **the**; it never changes. But all verbs and many other words have more than one form. For example, the verb **go** has five forms (**go, goes, going, went, gone**). We give names to the different forms of a word. For example, **goes** is the **-s** form of the verb **go**.

FORMATION   one or more verbs together in a sentence. For example, the Present Continuous is a verb formation.

PREPOSITION   examples of prepositions are: **at, in, on, under** and **with**. They go before noun phrases.

QUESTION   a sentence which asks for information. For example, **Has he worked hard?**

STATEMENT   a sentence which gives information. For example, **He has worked hard** and **He has not worked hard.**

SUBJECT   every sentence has a subject. It tells us what the sentence is about. For example, in **He has worked**, the subject is **He**.

TENSE   a verb form which tells us something about time. The first word of the verb of the sentence is always either present tense or past tense. For example, **I have been working** is in present tense because **have** is present.

Note: 'Tense' is not the same thing as 'time'. 'Tense' is a grammar word. 'Time' is not.

VERB we use this word for two meanings:
1 a type of word (like 'noun' or 'preposition'). For example **do, have, run, believe** and **learn**.
2 a part of the sentence (like 'subject' or 'clause'). For example, in **I have been working very hard**, the verb is **have been working**.

1

THE BASIC SENTENCE

The basic parts of every sentence are its subject and its verb so it is important that you can recognise them. The form of the verb can depend on the subject.

1.1 The sentence (PBEG 1)

Look at the words below. Are they sentences or not? Answer 'Yes' or 'No' and say why.

Example: She student.
Answer: No. (because there is no verb)

1 John a manager.
2 John is a manager.
3 John the manager of the shop.
4 John is the manager of the shop.
5 John works at the shop on the corner.
6 John at the shop on the corner of the street.
7 Works six days a week.
8 He works six days a week.
9 Some of my friends from America.
10 Some of my friends are from America.
11 Some of my friends from America have come to visit me.
12 Are you a student?
13 I student.
14 I a student.
15 I am a student.
16 I work.
17 Am working very hard.
18 He very happy about it.
19 Is he happy about it?
20 He is very happy about it.

1.2 The subject (PBEG 1; 2)

Find the subject in the sentences below.

Example: The new factory is opening tomorrow.
Answer: The new factory.

1 Maria is working at the factory.
2 The factory makes spare parts for cars.
3 My friends work at the factory too.
4 Are they going to work today?

5   Some people never learn.
6   Are you and John having a good time on holiday?
7   Rivers have always been important in the history of mankind.
8   The Nile is the longest river in Africa.
9   It is very important to millions of people.
10 My luggage has been lost.
11 Computers make learning more interesting.
12 Oranges and apples are both very cheap here.

1.3 *The verb* (PBEG 1; 3)

Find the verb in the sentences below.

Example: The new factory is opening tomorrow.
Answer: is opening.

1   Are you a student?
2   Yes, I am.
3   My phone number is 661-8939.
4   John plays football.
5   He is playing football now.
6   He has been playing football the whole afternoon.
7   The best match in the World Cup was Brazil v. France.
8   Are they the players who were sent off?
9   I like coffee.
10 It helps me to wake up in the morning.
11 I would like some coffee now.
12 I have seen that film three times.
13 He was born in 1963.
14 My wallet has been stolen.
15 We often think about you.
16 The letter should have arrived by now.

1.4 *Singular or plural?* (PBEG 2)

Find the word that decides whether the subject is singular or plural.

Example: One of my days at school
Answer: One – singular (only one day)
Example: My father and my brother
Answer: and – plural (more than one)

1   The best student in the class
2   The best students in the class
3   One of the best students in the class
4   The best student in the class and the worst student in the class
5   Some of the best students in the class
6   Money
7   Money problems
8   Problems with money
9   Travelling

10 Travelling to foreign countries
11 The result of yesterday's match
12 The results of yesterday's matches
13 The result of yesterday's matches
14 Tomorrow's programme
15 The car doors
16 The doors of the car
17 The company's Managing Director
18 The company's employees

NOTE For more practice with singular or plural, look at Extra Exercises 7.

1.5 Subject and verb agreement (PBEG 2; 4.1)

Fill in the gap with the correct form of the verb in brackets.

Example: He _____ (do) not know what to do.
Answer: He <u>does</u> not know what to do.

Look at this. My cassette recorder (**1**) _____ (have) stopped working.
I (**2**) _____ (think) it (**3**) _____ (have) been broken. Who
(**4**) _____ (do) you think broke it? When I (**5**) _____ (find) them, I'll
kill them.

England (**6**) _____ (have) a temperate climate. It (**7**) _____ (do) not
get very cold in winter. If you (**8**) _____ (go) there in the summer, you
(**9**) _____ (do) not need many warm clothes. But people still
(**10**) _____ (have) to have a jacket because the weather (**11**) _____
(change) from day to day. You (**12**) _____ (will) also need an umbrella. If
someone (**13**) _____ (forget) their umbrella, it always (**14**) _____
(rain). If you (**15**) _____ (have) forgotten to buy one before you
(**16**) _____ (leave) on holiday, remember that most clothes shops
(**17**) _____ (sell) them. An umbrella (**18**) _____ (do) not cost very
much and it (**19**) _____ (be) easy to carry. But be careful! Don't lose it
when it (**20**) _____ (be) not raining.

1.6 Agreement with the verb *be* – present tense
(PBEG 2; 4.2)

Fill in the gap with am, is or are.

Example: Where _____ the children?
Answer: Where <u>are</u> the children?

My name (**1**) _____ Peter. I (**2**) _____ 23 years old. I (**3**) _____
married. My wife (**4**) _____ called Maria. We (**5**) _____ very happy.
I work at a university. It (**6**) _____ a good job. My friend John
(**7**) _____ there with me. We (**8**) _____ computer technicians. John

(9) _____ very good at this job. I (10) _____ not bad at it either.

11 _____ Maria coming to the party this evening?
12 _____ Maria and you coming to the party this evening?
13 Sorry, _____ I taking your seat?
14 Foreign languages _____ often difficult to learn.
15 The best way to learn foreign languages _____ to travel.
16 Pollution _____ not only a modern problem.

1.7 Agreement with the verb – *be* past tense (PBEG 2; 4.2)

Fill in the gap with **was** *or* **were.**

Example: Where _____ the children yesterday?
Answer: Where <u>were</u> the children yesterday?

1 I _____ born in 1966.
2 My wife _____ born in the same year.
3 My wife and I _____ at school together.
4 We _____ good students.
5 When he _____ at school, John did very well in maths.
6 Why _____ the shops in the High Street closed yesterday?
7 The shops in the High Street _____ closed because it _____ a holiday.
8 The company's Managing Director _____ very rich.
9 The company's employees _____ not very rich.
10 The car doors _____ locked.
11 The doors of the car _____ locked.
12 One of the players _____ very good.

NOTE For more practice with verb forms after singular and plural subjects, look at Extra Exercises 7.

2

MORE ABOUT THE BASIC SENTENCE

We use **not** to make a negative sentence. We use an apostrophe (**n't**) for short forms. The subject and verb usually come before the other parts of a sentence, but the exact order depends on the type of sentence. Word order is very important in English.

2.1 Word order (PBEG 7)

Change the order of the words or groups of words to make a correct sentence.

Example: am / very happy / I
Answer: I am very happy.

1 went / last week / to see the doctor / I
2 not / feeling / I / was / well
3 a terrible headache / had / I
4 headaches / never usually / get / I
5 me / asked / about the headache / the doctor
6 a number of questions / he / asked
7 this headache / start / ? / when did
8 keep you awake at night / the headache / ? / does
9 like this / how long have you / ? / been feeling
10 what to do / told / me / he
11 this medicine / three times a day / take
12 work / do not / too hard
13 to the chemist / went / I / to get the medicine
14 the medicine / for four days / took / I
15 felt / I / after that / better
16 not / since that time / I / been to the doctor / have

2.2 Sentences with **not** (PBEG 5)

*Answer the questions below with sentences using **not**.*

Example: Have you found something?
Answer: I have not (haven't) found anything.

1 Does he play tennis?
2 Have you got a lot of money?
3 Has it been raining?
4 Are you doing many courses this term?
5 Do fish eat fruit?
6 Did you arrive on time?

7 Were they watching TV?
8 Have you been working hard?

2.3 More sentences with **not** (PBEG 5)

*Complete the sentence, using **not** and the word in brackets.*

Example: I can drive but I _____ (swim)
Answer: I can drive but I cannot (can't) swim.

1 John plays tennis but he _____ (football).
2 These shops sell food but they _____ (drinks).
3 Maria passed the maths exam but she _____ (physics).
4 She knows Maria but she _____ (John).
5 I went to Italy but I _____ (France).
6 They have finished the bedroom but they _____ (living room).
7 It has been raining but it _____ (snowing).
8 The glasses were broken but _____ (plates).

2.4 Short forms – reading (PBEG 6)

What are the full forms of the underlined words?

Example: What's your name?
Answer: is

1 This exercise isn't very difficult.
2 It's easy.
3 It won't take much time.
4 I think I'll be finished in five minutes.
5 I've answered four questions already.
6 John's already done all of them.
7 He's going home now.
8 He's got a new car.

NOTE For more practice with the meaning of apostrophe **s** ('s), and with
the meaning of apostrophe **d** ('d), look at Extra Exercises 1 and 2.

2.5 Short forms – writing (PBEG 6)

Rewrite these sentences using short forms where you can.

Example: What is your name?
Answer: What's your name?

1 I do not know if John has arrived yet.
2 I will not be able to attend tomorrow.
3 I will see you when you have finished.
4 She is going to the party but she is not staying late.

2.6 Types of sentences (PBEG 1.2; 18; 7.1)

Is the sentence a statement, a question or an imperative?

1 It is always difficult to find a good job.
2 Is money the most important thing?
3 Should you look for something interesting?
4 I know how difficult this is.
5 You should be careful.
6 Never take a job just because the pay is good.
7 You may find that you are unhappy.
8 Always try to find out about the job first.

2.7 Subject and verb (PBEG 7)

Find the word or words which form the subject and the word or words which form the verb.

Example: My cousin has always had good luck in life.
Answer: Subject: My cousin   Verb: has . . . had

1 Football is one of my favourite sports.
2 Do you like football?
3 It really is a very exciting game.
4 Why don't you try it some time?
5 We are going to have a practice match after school today.
6 We always have a practice match on Thursdays.
7 You can come along if you like.
8 The bank opened at nine o'clock.
9 Ten minutes later, the robbers arrived in their van.
10 They waited until there were no customers in the bank.
11 Then they went inside.
12 The bank clerks didn't stop them.
13 They were very frightened.
14 They gave the robbers all the money.
15 Outside the bank, one of the robbers was waiting in the van.
16 At 9.15, the other robbers came out with the money.

3

QUESTION WORDS

Question words ask for information. They go at the beginning of a sentence. We put a question mark (?) at the end of the question.

3.1 Word order (PBEG 7; 8)

Change the order of the words or groups of words to make a correct sentence.
Example: are you late / ? / why
Answer: Why are you late?

1 are you going / ? / where
2 were they doing / what / last night / ?
3 does he play tennis / often / ? / how
4 ? / how / are you / tall
5 university / did he go to / ? / which
6 does that painting cost / ? / much / how
7 like / is the weather / ? / what
8 kind / ? / of car is it / what

3.2 Recognising question words (PBEG 8)

Find the part of the sentence that is the answer to the question word on the left.
Example: What . . .? I bought the expensive cassette recorder.
Answer: the expensive cassette recorder.
Example: Which . . .? I bought the expensive cassette recorder.
Answer: the expensive

1	Who . . .?	The post office workers are on strike.
2	How long . . .?	They have been on strike for two months.
3	How many months . . .?	They have been on strike for two months.
4	Where . . .?	Millions of letters are lying in post offices everywhere.
5	What . . .?	Millions of letters are lying in post offices everywhere.
6	How many . . .?	Millions of letters are lying in post offices everywhere.
7	What . . . for?	The managers use part-time staff for extra work.
8	Who . . .?	The workers do not like the part-time system.

9	What . . .?	The workers do not like the part-time system.
10	Which . . .?	The workers do not like the part-time system.
11	Who . . .?	They are angry because they want the extra work themselves.
12	Why . . .?	They are angry because they want the extra work themselves.
13	What . . .?	They want the extra work to earn more money.
14	Why . . .?	They want the extra work to earn more money.
15	Who . . .?	They want the extra work to earn more money.
16	How much . . .?	A postman's wage is only £110 every week.
17	How many . . .?	A postman's wage is only £110 every week.
18	How often . . .?	A postman's wage is only £110 every week.
19	Whose . . .?	A postman's wage is only £110 every week.
20	What kind . . .?	This is a very low wage.
21	How low . . .?	This is a very low wage.
22	Who . . .?	The managers and workers had a very angry meeting yesterday.
23	What kind . . .?	The managers and workers had a very angry meeting yesterday.
24	When . . .?	The managers and workers had a very angry meeting yesterday.

3.3 Using question words (PBEG 8)

Look at the part of the sentence in italics. This part is the answer to a question. How does the question begin?

Example: That car can go at *150 mph.*

Answer: How fast . . .?

1 He is *at least seventy years old.*
2 He was born *a very long time ago.*
3 He had *three* brothers and two sisters.
4 He went to primary school *in Liverpool.*
5 It was a *very good* school.
6 He did *very well* with his studies at school.
7 He did *very* well *indeed.*

8. He could have gone *to university*.
9. But he didn't *because of money*.
10. His parents had *very little* money.
11. Instead, he joined *the merchant navy*.
12. On his first trip, he went *to Brazil*.
13. Brazil was *6,000 miles* from Liverpool.
14. He felt *very homesick and lonely*.
15. The return journey took *three months*.
16. *His second* trip was to Australia.
17. It was a *terrible* journey.
18. It was a terrible journey *because the sea was very rough*.
19. But *after a year or so*, he got used to the life.
20. He went to Brazil *twice a year* for the next forty years.
21. He has been round the world *six* times.
22. He retired from the sea *twenty years ago*.

4

MAKING QUESTIONS

In most questions, the first word of the verb goes before the subject. The first word of the verb is also important for short answers and tag questions.

4.1 Word order (PBEG 9; 13)

Change the order of the words or groups of words to make a correct sentence.

Example: you / ? / do / her / know
Answer: Do you know her?

1 do / ? / do / you / how
2 you / going / are / ? / where
3 ? / like / you / tomatoes / do
4 do / tomatoes / like / ? / why / you
5 the match / ? / finish / will / when
6 they / come from / ? / do / where
7 didn't / ? / me / tell / why / you
8 does / belong to / that car / ? / who
9 a telephone / is there / ? / near here
10 you / do / ? / when we arrive / know
11 you / have / what / ? / been doing
12 tell me / you / ? / the way to the bank / could
13 where he is / ? / you / know / do
14 on Saturday / ? / we / have to come / do
15 where / he lives / know / I
16 he hasn't come / wonder / I / why

4.2 Making questions (PBEG 9; 10; 13)

Fill in the gap in the sentence on the left to make a correct question for the answer on the right.

Example: When _____ happen?   It happened yesterday.
Answer: When <u>did it</u> happen?

1	Where _____ go yesterday?	I went to school.
2	_____ come to the party?	Yes, I will if I have the time.
3	Who _____ the race?	John won it easily.
4	_____ borrow your pencil?	Yes, but I want it back.
5	_____ seen that new film yet?	No I haven't, but I'm going to.
6	When _____ up this morning?	I got up at half past six.
7	Who _____?	He told Maria.

8	Who _____ about it?	John told her.	
9	Why _____ driving so slowly?	There's a police car behind us.	
10	Where _____ from?	He comes from Manchester.	
11	When _____ that report?	I'll finish it today, I think.	
12	Which books _____?	I need all the ones on the shelf.	
13	Who _____ this glass?	I broke it. I'm very sorry.	
14	Why _____ finish that report?	Because I was too tired.	
15	Do _____ what the time is?	It's nearly eleven o'clock.	
16	Could _____ me when the plane _____?	It leaves at 16.45.	

4.3 More questions to make (PBEG 9)

A passport officer is talking to a foreign student. Use the words below to make complete questions.

Example: What passport number
Answer: What is your passport number?

1	What name	**5**	Which country from
2	Where live	**6**	Why come here
3	What address	**7**	Where study
4	When born	**8**	How long stay

4.4 Polite questions (PBEG 13)

Do exercise 4.3 again, but this time the passport officer is very polite. How does he ask the questions?

Example: What passport number
Answer: Could you tell me what your passport number is?

4.5 What can you ask? (PBEG 8; 9; 10; 13)

Make a suitable question for each situation described below.

1 You meet a friend. She is looking for a car to buy.
   Have . . . ?

2 You need to borrow a little money from a friend.
   Can . . . ?

3 You are in a foreign country and do not speak the language. You go into a shop.
   . . . English?

4 Your friend is ill. You go to see him.
   . . . feeling?

5 You meet a friend. She has just come back from her holiday.
   . . . a good time?

6 You are in a tourist information office. Ask about the price of the ticket on the airport bus.
... the bus to the airport cost?

7 Now you are on the airport bus. Ask a passenger when it arrives at the airport.
Do you know when . . .?

8 You want some money but the banks are closed. You ask at tourist information.
When . . .?

9 You are looking for the bank. You ask somebody on the street.
Could you . . .?

10 You are making a drink for a friend.
... tea or coffee?

11 You want a meeting with Maria. You ask her.
Can . . . on Friday?

12 You are with a group of friends. You decide to go for a drink. Ask if anybody wants to come with you.
Who . . . with me?

13 You want the no. 89 bus, but perhaps you are at the wrong bus stop. You ask the person next to you.
Do . . . if the no. 89 . . . here?

14 You have just given your opinion. You want to know if other people agree with you or not.
... think?

15 Your watch is being repaired in a shop. You want to know when you can collect it.
... be ready?

16 You are looking for the accommodation office in a big university building. You ask a student.
Do . . . which floor . . . on?

4.6 *Short answers* (PBEG 11)

Answer the question with a short answer. Begin with 'Yes' or 'No'.
Example: Is your name John Smith?
Answer: No, it isn't.
Example: Can you speak English?
Answer: Yes, I can.

1 Are you a student?
2 Have you been studying English for long?
3 Is it necessary to do a lot of homework?
4 Was English difficult for you at first?

5 Did you have to study hard?
6 Who first taught you English?
7 Who's the best student in your class?
8 Do you have to go to lessons in the evening?
9 Have you seen the film 'Star Wars'?
10 Can you help me, please?
11 What's your favourite subject at school?
12 Will you be at home this afternoon?

4.7 Tag questions (PBEG 12)

Complete the sentence using a tag question.
Example: It's a lovely day, _____?
Answer: It's a lovely day, isn't it?

1 It was a wonderful match, _____?
2 They weren't very good, _____?
3 He's the captain, _____?
4 They're the best in the country, _____?
5 They can find their own way home, _____?
6 She's thinking of going to Australia, _____?
7 He should go to a doctor, _____?
8 She couldn't have arrived already, _____?
9 He doesn't like studying English, _____?
10 Teachers always hate marking homework, _____?
11 They won't have got there yet, _____?
12 You spent five years in China, _____?
13 But now you live in Africa, _____?
14 You've been living there for years, _____?
15 She never found her money, _____?
16 Taxi drivers often work at night, _____?

NOTE For more practice with tag questions, look at Extra Exercises 3.

5

VERB FORMS

English verbs have very few forms. This section gives you practice in producing them correctly. Be careful with the spelling and with irregular verbs.

5.1 The -s form (PBEG 14; appendix 5)

Fill in the gap with the -s form of the verb in brackets.
Example: She _____ (like) watching TV.
Answer: She <u>likes</u> watching TV.

John Smith is a teacher. He (1) _____ (work) at the local school. He (2) _____ (teach) maths there. But he's a student in his free time; he (3) _____ (study) physics. He (4) _____ (go) to work every day in his red sports car. He (5) _____ (look) after his car very carefully. He (6) _____ (wash) it every weekend so that it is always clean. He never (7) _____ (drive) very fast in it, but it is a fast car and his wife (8) _____ (worry) about his safety.

5.2 The -ing form (PBEG 14; appendix 6)

Fill in the gap with the -ing form of the verb in brackets.
Example: I am _____ (work) late this week.
Answer: I am <u>working</u> late this week.

1 When are they _____ (come)?
2 They are _____ (arrive) at about eight o'clock.
3 When are they _____ (go)?
4 They are _____ (leave) for Spain tomorrow.
5 I think they're _____ (travel) by train.
6 Stop _____ (worry)!
7 I don't mind _____ (walk) to the station.
8 Stop _____ (run)! You'll fall.
9 Look! The bus is _____ (stop).
10 He's _____ (hope) to get here today.
11 I'm _____ (die) to meet him.
12 They were _____ (have) lunch when I arrived.
13 How long have you been _____ (attend) English classes.
14 . It's _____ (rain) outside; you'll need an umbrella.
15 And it seems to be _____ (get) colder.

16 I saw a man _____ (lie) in the road.

17 Thank you for _____ (fix) the TV.

18 They are _____ (offer) their house to us for a week.

19 He's _____ (win) the race.

20 We are _____ (look) forward to _____ (see) you.

21 They're _____ (put) up the bus fares.

22 The cost of _____ (live) is _____ (rise).

5.3 *The past tense form* (PBEG 14; 16.3; appendices 7,10)

Fill in the gap with the past tense form of the verb in brackets.

Example: We _____ (work) hard yesterday.

Answer: We <u>worked</u> hard yesterday.

1 What _____ (do) you do yesterday?

2 I _____ (make) a cake.

3 First, I _____ (bake) it in the oven for an hour.

4 Then, I _____ (leave) it to cool.

5 Then, I _____ (fill) it with cream.

6 I _____ (give) it to my guests this morning.

7 I _____ (put) it on a large plate . . .

8 and _____ (carry) it through to the living room.

9 I _____ (cut) it with a knife.

10 I _____ (offer) everybody a piece.

11 They _____ (love) it.

12 They _____ (think) it _____ (taste) delicious.

13 I _____ (feel) very proud of myself.

14 I _____ (buy) everything for the cake from a local shop.

15 It only _____ (cost) £1 to make.

16 I _____ (have) an accident last week.

17 A car _____ (hit) me.

18 I _____ (fall) down and _____ (break) my arm.

19 The driver _____ (take) me to hospital.

20 They _____ (keep) me there for three hours.

21 They _____ (fit) me with a plaster for my arm.

22 Then they _____ (let) me go.

I (**23**) _____ (go) to the cinema yesterday. I (**24**) _____ (see) a good film there. It (**25**) _____ (be) a Japanese film. The film (**26**) _____ (take) a very long time. It (**27**) _____ (last) more than two and a half hours. But it (**28**) _____ (be) never boring. In the film, three people (**29**) _____ (tell) the same story. But each person (**30**) _____ (have) different memories of what (**31**) _____ (happen). The people

(32) _____ (speak) in Japanese, but I (33) _____ (understand) everything because the film (34) _____ (be) subtitled in English.

5.4 The past participle form
(PBEG 14; 16.5; appendices 7,10)

Fill in the gap with the past participle form of the verb in brackets.

Example: I had _____ (hope) to see you there.

Answer: I had <u>hoped</u> to see you there.

1   My brother has _____ (lend) me his car.
2   I'm afraid it was _____ (send) to the wrong address.
3   I've _____ (lose) my wallet.
4   He has _____ (play) in every match this season.
5   The painting was _____ (sell) for a million pounds.
6   It was _____ (buy) by an American.
7   The police have _____ (catch) the robbers.
8   Have you _____ (get) your books with you?
9   I don't think we've _____ (meet) before.
10 We were _____ (teach) three languages at our school.
11 The population of the world has now _____ (reach) six billion.
12 I think I've _____ (leave) my bag on the bus.
13 He's _____ (live) there all his life.
14 I've _____ (know) him for about a year.
15 Who's _____ (take) my bag?
16 Maria has _____ (go) to Australia.
17 I've never _____ (be) to Australia.
18 Have you _____ (do) the washing-up yet?
19 We can't watch that programme; the TV is _____ (break).
20 I hadn't _____ (see) him for six years.
21 That watch was _____ (give) to me by my grandfather.
22 Have you ever _____ (be) water-skiing?
23 They must have _____ (have) a wonderful time on holiday.
24 Dates have been _____ (grow) in Arabia for centuries.
25 It was your fault. You should have _____ (be) more careful.
26 All these products are _____ (make) in Hong Kong.
27 You should have _____ (tell) me. Then I could have _____ (help) you.

6

VERB FORMS IN VERB FORMATIONS

We can use the verb forms for many different purposes. In particular, we can use them next to each other, in a strict order, to make many different verb formations. When we do this, auxiliary verbs are very important. This section gives you practice at putting verbs together correctly.

6.1 *Word order* (PBEG 7; 15; 17; 18)

Change the order of the words or groups of words to make a correct sentence.
Example: have / working hard / been / I
Answer: I have been working hard.

1 is / terrible / the weather today
2 been / it has / raining / for ten hours
3 stronger and stronger / getting / the wind / is
4 blown down / have / some trees / been
5 had / have / accidents / lots of drivers
6 all ferryboats / been / cancelled / have
7 took / five hours / the last ferry journey
8 was / waiting for two hours / outside the harbour / it
9 too rough to go inside / the sea / was
10 feeling / the passengers / were / very sick
11 from side to side / was / the boat / rocking
12 on that boat / travelling / was / I
13 not / enjoy myself / I / did
14 had / I / been feeling well / not
15 after the journey / much worse / felt / I
16 gone / have / I should / by plane
17 much better / been / that would / have
18 shall / on a ferryboat again / never travel / I
19 give / some advice / let me / you
20 by ferryboat in bad weather / go / not / do

6.2 *The verb* **be** (PBEG 16)

Fill in the gap with **be, being** *or* **been**.
Example: I've _____ to see the doctor.
Answer: I've <u>been</u> to see the doctor.

1 You should have _____ more careful.
2 You should always _____ careful when you cross the road.

3 The road is _____ repaired.

4 It has _____ repaired three times before.

5 Don't _____ so stupid again.

6 _____ careful on the roads is important in a busy town.

7 So _____ careful, and you will never _____ involved in an accident again.

6.3 *The correct auxiliary – present* (PBEG 17)

*Fill in the gap with **do/does**, **have/has** or **is/are**.*

Example: How many children _____ you have?

Answer: How many children <u>do</u> you have? (**do/does** because **have** is base form and **do** – not **does** – because the subject is 'you')
subject is you)

1 I see that the Smith children _____ missing again.

2 _____ you know where they are?

3 They _____ not coming to school today.

4 They _____ missed a whole week of school.

5 They say they _____ going to come next week.

6 _____ you seen them lately?

7 Their mother _____ not know that they _____ been away.

8 _____ she been told about this?

9 Who _____ going to talk to her about it?

10 Mr Jones _____ been trying to talk to her for weeks now.

11 But her phone _____ always engaged.

NOTE For practice with the meaning of apostrophe **s** ('**s**) for **is**, **has** or genitive, look at Extra Exercises 1.

6.4 *The correct auxiliary – past* (PBEG 17)

*Fill in the gap with **did**, **had** or **was/were**.*

Example: What _____ he doing at the time?

Answer: What <u>was</u> he doing at the time? (**was/were** because of the **-ing** form verb, and **was** – not **were** – because the subject is '**HE**')

1 The train _____ not arrive on time this morning.

2 I _____ not mind at first . . .

3 because I _____ reading a very interesting book.

4 I _____ not notice that the station was very quiet.

5 I _____ been waiting at the station for an hour . . .

6 when I realised that something strange _____ happening.

7 When I looked around, I _____ surprised to find that everybody else _____ left.

8 Then I realised that I _____ not seen any trains at all.

9 I found the station staff; they _____ having tea.

10 '_____ n't you hear the announcement?' they asked.

11 They told me they _____ announced the cancellation of all trains for the day half an hour before.

NOTE For practice with the meaning of apostrophe **d** ('**d**) for **had** or **would**, look at Extra Exercises 2.

For practice with the difference between **were, we're** and **where**, look at Extra Exercises 9.

6.5 *The correct verb form* (PBEG 15; 17)

Fill in the gap with the correct form of the verb in brackets.

Example: I have _____ (go) to lunch.

Answer: I have <u>gone</u> to lunch. (because the auxiliary is **have**)

Dinosaurs were some of the biggest animals that have ever (**1**) _____ (live) on the earth. They lived here millions of years ago. No man has ever (**2**) _____ (see) a dinosaur. Man did not (**3**) _____ (appear) until much later. All the dinosaurs had (**4**) _____ (die) out by then.

But scientists have (**5**) _____ (discover) a lot about them. If Early Man had been (**6**) _____ (live) at that time, he would have (**7**) _____ (be) very afraid of them. Some of them must (**8**) _____ (have) (**9**) _____ (be) very, very big. Some of them were able to (**10**) _____ (run) fast too. A few of them used to (**11**) _____ (eat) other dinosaurs.

There is a lot that scientists still don't (**12**) _____ (know). They are always (**13**) _____ (try) to (**14**) _____ (find) new information. Lately, scientists have been (**15**) _____ (study) a new idea. The idea is that dinosaurs might have (**16**) _____ (have) warm blood – just like us!

They are also (**17**) _____ (try) to (**18**) _____ (find) the answer to a big mystery. Why did the dinosaurs (**19**) _____ (die) out so suddenly? It is a difficult problem, but they will probably (**20**) _____ (arrive) at the answer in the end.

NOTE For more practice in choosing the correct verb form after **be**, look at Extra Exercises 6.

7

CONSTRUCTING VERB FORMATIONS

Verb formations can be one word or more than one word. If they have more than one word, we use auxiliary verbs. This section gives you practice with how to make the different verb formations. The next two sections give you practice with when to use them.

7.1 *Present simple* (PBEG 19)

Use the words in brackets and the present simple formation to complete the sentence. Be careful with questions and negatives.

Example: _____ (I like) coffee. Can I have tea instead?
Answer: I don't like coffee. Can I have tea instead?

1 How many languages _____ (he know)?
2 _____ (you live) in the centre of town?
3 _____ (she like) meat. It gives her a headache.
4 Manchester is very wet. _____ (it rain) more than 200 days a year.
5 _____ (it have) a population of about half a million.
6 _____ (she eat) a lot of fruit.
7 She used to walk to work but now _____ (she drive).
8 How often _____ (she visit) her parents?

7.2 *Past simple* (PBEG 21)

Use the words in brackets and the past simple formation to complete the sentence. Be careful with questions and negatives.

Example: How _____ (you know) my name? I've never seen you
            before.
Answer: How did you know my name? I've never seen you before.

1 _____ (we arrange) to meet outside the cinema last night, but you weren't there.
2 _____ (I meet) you last night because I had to take my mother to hospital.
3 Your mother! What _____ (happen) to her?
4 _____ (she fall) and broke her leg.
5 I phoned for an ambulance but _____ (it come) so I took her myself.
6 You've got a car! _____ (I know) you had a car!

7 When _____ (you get) it?

8 _____ (I expect) to see you at the party but you weren't there. Why _____ (you come)?

9 When Columbus _____ (cross) the Atlantic, _____ (he think) he would find India. _____ (He know) anything about America. It was a big surprise to him.

7.3 *Present continuous* (PBEG 22)

Complete the sentence with one verb from the list below and any other words necessary. Use the present continuous formation. Be careful with negatives and questions.

work go write look come use do get on

Example: Where _____ you _____?

Answer: Where <u>are you going</u>?

I **(1)** _____ this letter to thank you for the lovely present. It's a very nice typewriter. I **(2)** _____ it now. How **(3)** _____ you _____ in your new job? **(4)** _____ hard? I hope everything **(5)** _____ well. Maria **(6)** _____ forward to visiting you next month. When **(7)** _____ to visit us? We **(8)** _____ not _____ very much at the moment (business is slow), so any time would be fine.

7.4 *Past continuous* (PBEG 23)

Complete the sentence with one verb from the list below and any other necessary words. Use the past continuous formation. Be careful with questions and negatives.

do hope feel go

Example: Why _____ he _____ to the bank?

Answer: Why <u>was he going</u> to the bank?

1 When Columbus discovered America, _____ to find India.

2 The sailors on the ship _____ sick because they didn't have enough vitamin C.

3 Where _____ when I stopped you?

4 What _____ before they turned on the TV?

7.5 *Present perfect simple* (PBEG 24)

Use the words in brackets and the present perfect simple formation to complete the sentence. Be careful with questions and negatives.

Example: _____ (I see) you for years. What a lovely surprise!

Answer: <u>I have not seen</u> you for years. What a lovely surprise!

1 _____ (they help) hundreds of old people.

2 _____ (you ever be) to America?

3 Where's John? _____ (he go) to the Economics Department.
4 Why _____ (you do) your homework? I told you it was important.
5 John's bicycle looks very old. How long _____ (he have) it?
6 If _____ (you see) that film, you're really missing something.
7 No, _____ (I eat) Chinese food before, but I would like to try it.
8 Ah, there you are at last! Where _____ (you be) all this time?

7.6 Past perfect simple (PBEG 26)

Complete the sentence with one verb from the list below and any other necessary words. Use the past perfect simple formation. Be careful with negatives and questions.

know   expect   see   finish
Example: I _____ him since 1986.
Answer: I had not seen him since 1986.

1 They _____ when I arrived.
2 How long _____ each other before they got married?
3 I _____ to get so much money. It was a wonderful surprise.
4 _____ these animals before, but only on TV.

7.7 Present perfect continuous (PBEG 24)

Use the words in brackets and the present perfect continuous formation to complete the sentence. Be careful with questions and negatives.

Example: Hello. I hope _____ (you wait) long.
Answer: Hello. I hope you have not been waiting long.

1 _____ (I come) to this place for years.
2 _____ (she play) the guitar for only a few months and she's already very good.
3 I haven't seen you for ages. What _____ (you do)?
4 How long _____ (you wait) here?
5 He says _____ (he think) about it but he still hasn't decided.
6 I wonder what _____ (they talk) to each other about.
7 The children _____ (have) a wonderful time with that toy.
8 It's a terrible situation! Why _____ (they try) to do something about it?

7.8 *Past perfect continuous* (PBEG 26)

Complete the sentence with one verb from the list below and any other necessary words. Use the past perfect continuous formation. Be careful with negatives and questions.

do   feel   live   steal

Example: I wanted to know what she _____ (say).
Answer: I wanted to know what she <u>had been saying.</u>

1   They _____ things from the company for five years.
2   _____ in the house for very long when I had to move again.
3   The police asked me what _____ for the past hour.
4   I _____ very well for several days, so I called the doctor.

8

PAST OR PRESENT

This section gives you practice in deciding which tense to use.

The first word of the verb formation always shows either the present tense (with the base form or the **-s** form) or the past tense (with the past tense form). Very generally, the meanings of the two tenses are:
– present: 'here and now', 'not finished' or 'important for now';
– past: 'there and then', 'finished' or 'not important for now'.
PBEG 20 and 21.2 will give you a general idea of the difference and some examples.

8.1 The verb do (PBEG 19; 63.8)

Fill in the gap with **do, does** *or* **did**.

Example: Ah, you're here. When _____ you get here?
Answer: Ah, you're here. When <u>did</u> you get here?

1   _____ you two know each other already?
2   _____ you know each other before you met here?
3   Why _____ not you tell me you were coming?
4   _____ anybody know where the toilets are?
5   Where _____ you find that beautiful skirt?
6   Why _____ not we go to the cinema? You'll like the film.
7   not use that machine. It _____ n't work.
8   I _____ not use to find work so tiring, but now I do.

We (**9**) _____ not do our homework last night. The teacher told us that we (**10**) _____ not have to do it if we (**11**) _____ n't want to.

8.2 The verb be (PBEG 22.2; 23.2; 63.8)

Fill in the gap with **am, is, are, was** *or* **were**.

Example: I _____ very happy at the moment.
Answer: I <u>am</u> very happy at the moment.

(If you are not sure about the difference between **am/is/are**, and between **was/were**, look at PBEG 4.2)

1   There _____ an open air concert on today in the park.
2   A very famous band _____ playing.
3   I _____ going to see it if I have time.
4   The band _____ supposed to be very good.
5   They _____ on last week in the city theatre.
6   The critics in last week's newspapers said that they _____ very good.

7 They said that the band _____ improving all the time.

8 People at the concert _____ surprised by the music they played.

9 It _____ not the kind of music they usually played.

10 _____ they going to play the same kind of music this time?

11 I _____ looking forward to finding out.

12 I _____ wondering if you would like to come too.

8.3 The verb **have** (PBEG 25; 40.2)

*Fill in the gap with **have, has** or **had**.*

Example: _____ you finished that exercise yet?

Answer: Have you finished that exercise yet? (because it is important
for now)

1 I'm very happy because I _____ just had a wonderful surprise.

2 I _____ just been given a lot of money.

3 The money was my uncle's, but he _____ decided he doesn't need it.

4 My uncle _____ a business until three years ago.

5 Since that time, he _____ not done very much.

6 He _____ been trying to write a book.

7 Anyway, yesterday, a lawyer _____ some news for him.

8 There was some money from the business that he _____ forgotten about.

8.4 Verbs in general (PBEG 22.2; 23.2; 25.2; 26.2; 63.8)

*Fill in the gap with the base form, the **-s** form or the past form of the verb in brackets.*

Example: I never _____ (work) on Sundays.

Answer: I never work on Sundays. (base form)

1 How _____ (do) you do? I'm very pleased to meet you.

2 _____ (do) you see the football match last night?

3 I _____ (know) him when he was just a small boy.

I can't understand him. He (4) _____ (have) a strange accent and he (5) _____ (speak) very fast.

Last year I (6) _____ (go) to work on foot but now I (7) _____ (walk).

He (8) _____ (break) his leg when he (9) _____ (have) the accident.

Why are you driving to the petrol station? There (10) _____ (be) no need to go there; we (11) _____ (fill) up the tank yesterday. Anyway, we (12) _____ (do) not have much time.

An interesting thing (**13**) _____ (happen) to me last night. I
(**14**) _____ (be) sitting in my room reading, when the phone
(**15**) _____ (ring). Immediately, I (**16**) _____ (put) down my book
and (**17**) _____ (answer) it. I (**18**) _____ (do) not usually
(**19**) _____ (run) to the phone so quickly. When I (**20**) _____ (be)
reading a book, I (**21**) _____ (hate) stopping. But this time I
(**22**) _____ (do) not mind. I think I (**23**) _____ (know) that it
(**24**) _____ (be) something important.

　　And I was right! The voice on the phone (**25**) _____ (belong) to an
old friend of mine. It was the first time I (**26**) _____ (have) heard from
her in three years. It (**27**) _____ (be) lovely to hear her voice after all
that time. We (**28**) _____ (have) arranged to meet tomorrow after I
(**29**) _____ (finish) classes. I can't wait to see what she (**30**) _____
(look) like now. I (**31**) _____ (wonder) if she (**32**) _____ (have)
changed.

8.5 *Past simple or present perfect* (PBEG 21.2; 25; 40.2)

*Use the verb in brackets and the past simple or the present perfect to complete
the sentence.*

Example: He _____ not _____ (do) his homework yet.
Answer: He <u>has</u> not <u>done</u> his homework yet. (present perfect)
Example: He _____ not _____ (do) his homework last night.
Answer: He <u>did</u> not <u>do</u> his homework last night. (past simple)

1 _____ you _____ (see) that film at the local cinema yet?
2 Yes, I _____ (see) that film lots of times.
3 I was so worried about it that I _____ not _____ (sleep) for
　　three days.
4 The last time I _____ (go) to England was in 1987.
5 I _____ (be) to England three times altogether.
6 I _____ not ever _____ (go) to Scotland.
7 Shakespeare _____ not ever _____ (go) to Scotland.
8 But surely you can't want to eat again. You _____ (have) three big
　　meals today.
9 I _____ (have) a big breakfast today.
10 Perhaps John _____ (get) lost. Shall I go out and look for him?
11 The newspaper _____ not _____ (arrive) again today, so I went
　　out and bought one.
12 You needn't do the washing-up. I _____ (do) it myself already.
13 _____ you _____ (enjoy) the film last night?
14 John _____ (promise) to take me to the match today.
15 John _____ (promise) to take me to the match today but it's
　　already half finished and he still _____ not _____ (arrive).

9

SIMPLE, CONTINUOUS AND PERFECT

This section gives you practice with choosing the correct verb formation for the meaning you want to communicate.

9.1 Present simple or present continuous
(PBEG 20; 22.2; 39.1)

Use the verb in brackets and the present simple or the present continuous formation to complete the sentence.

Example: Oh, sorry! _____ I _____ (ring) at a bad time?
Answer: Oh, sorry! <u>Am</u> I <u>ringing</u> at a bad time. (present continuous)
Example: London _____ (stand) on the River Thames.
Answer: London <u>stands</u> on the river Thames. (present simple)

1 How _____ you _____ (do)? I'm very pleased to meet you.

2 I'm an engineer. What about you? What _____ you _____ (do)?

3 Hello, Maria. I haven't seen you for a while. How _____ you _____ (do)?

4 What _____ you _____ (do) here? I thought you left hours ago.

5 What _____ you _____ (do) next weekend?

6 How many cigarettes _____ you _____ (smoke)?

7 I _____ (smoke) a lot today because I'm nervous.

8 How many hours _____ you _____ (work) every day?

9 Hey! Somebody stop him! He _____ (steal) my car.

10 I _____ (prefer) food which is not too hot.

11 That's a nice smell. Somebody _____ (cook) dinner.

12 We _____ (run) out of milk. Can you go and get some from the shop?

13 Japan _____ (lie) off the east coast of Asia.

14 All the teachers in this school _____ (speak) English.

15 The water _____ (boil). Now I can make the tea.

16 He _____ (know) a lot about computers.

17 Where _____ you _____ (go) for your holiday this year?

18 I _____ (want) to go to Egypt this summer.

19 This medicine _____ (taste) awful.

20 I _____ (stay) with my brother this weekend.

9.2 Present: simple/continuous/perfect
(PBEG 20; 22.2; 25; 39)

Use the verb in brackets and one of these three formations to complete the sentence. If you choose the present perfect, use the simple formation.

Example: Oh, no! I _____ (lose) my wallet.
Answer: Oh, no! I <u>have lost</u> my wallet. (present perfect)

1 Can you help me, please? I _____ (look) for the bank.
2 _____ you _____ (know) that student over there?
3 Yes, of course. I _____ (know) him for years.
4 He's Portuguese, like me. He _____ (come) from my home town.
5 I've got to go to the airport now. My brother _____ (come) from Portugal today.
6 This is my brother. He _____ (come) from Portugal today.
7 He _____ (collect) stamps ever since he was a small boy.
8 London is an old city. It _____ (stand) on the River Thames.
9 Be quiet and listen! The Director _____ (speak).
10 How long _____ it _____ (take) to get from here to London?
11 How long _____ you _____ (work) for the government?
12 I am very tired. I _____ not _____ (sleep) for three days.
13 I _____ (work) overtime all this week.
14 I _____ (go) to the football match tomorrow evening.
15 I _____ (have) this car since 1985.
16 Sorry, I can't talk now. I _____ (have) dinner.
17 That car _____ (look) nice, but I can't afford it.
18 The phone _____ (ring). Can somebody answer it?
19 I _____ never _____ (like) lemons. They _____ (have) such a sour taste.
20 She _____ (be) on the phone for half an hour now. Who _____ she _____ (talk) to?
21 We _____ (have) three meetings about this problem so far and we still _____ not _____ (decide) what to do.

9.3 Present perfect: simple or continuous
(PBEG 25.4; 39; 40.1)

Use the verb in brackets and the present perfect in simple or continuous formation to complete the sentence. In two of these sentences, both formations are possible.

Example: Hurry up! _____ not you _____ (finish) yet?
Answer: Hurry up! <u>Haven't</u> you <u>finished</u> yet? (present perfect simple)

1 I _____ always _____ (love) you.
2 I _____ (do) physics this term. It's very difficult.

3 I _____ (do) physics. I did it last term.

4 How long _____ you _____ (know) John?

5 He _____ not _____ (work) very hard this term.

6 He _____ never _____ (work) hard.

7 The pollution in this city _____ (get) worse every year.

8 _____ you ever _____ (do) the washing up?

9 _____ you _____ (do) the washing up yet?

10 _____ you _____ (do) the washing up for long? Let me help.

11 I _____ (fix) the car but it's taking a long time.

12 I _____ (fix) the car. Do you want to go for a drive?

9.4 Past simple or past continuous (PBEG 21; 23; 40.1)

Use the verb in brackets and the past simple or the past continuous to complete the sentence.

Example: I _____ (watch) TV when the phone _____ (ring).

Answer: I <u>was watching</u> (past continuous) TV when the phone <u>rang</u> (past simple).

1 We _____ not _____ (watch) so much TV when I was a girl.

2 We _____ (watch) TV when the power went off.

3 How _____ she _____ (manage) to do all that in one day?

4 Columbus _____ (discover) America in 1492.

5 I _____ not _____ (understand) that book.

6 We _____ (win) the match yesterday. The final result was 3–2.

We (**7**) _____ (win) the match yesterday when the referee (**8**) _____ (say) that he (**9**) _____ (stop) the game.

I (**10**) _____ (walk) along the road yesterday when I (**11**) _____ (meet) an old friend from home. She (**12**) _____ (look) for the post office.

We (**13**) _____ (go) outside to play football, but then we (**14**) _____ (look) out of the window and we (**15**) _____ (see) that it (**16**) _____ (snow) much too hard.

9.5 Past: simple/continuous/perfect
(PBEG 21.2; 23.2; 26.2; 40.1)

Use the verb in brackets and one of these three formations to complete the sentence.

Example: I _____ (work) in the library when I _____ (realise) it _____ (close).

Answer: I <u>was working</u> . . . <u>realised</u> it <u>had closed</u>.

Past continuous – past simple – past perfect

I am a doctor. I have to drive a lot in my job. I have been driving for twenty years. In all that time, the police (1) _____ never _____ (stop) me until last week. But last Tuesday, they (2) _____ (catch) me for speeding.

It was the afternoon. I (3) _____ (drive) fast because I was late. I (4) _____ (go) to the airport to meet a friend. I was late because a patient (5) _____ (telephone) just as I (6) _____ (leave) the house.

The police (7) _____ (wait) in the side road outside town. When they (8) _____ (see) me go past, they (9) _____ (drive) after me. Then they (10) _____ (stop) me. They told me that they (11) _____ (book) me for speeding.

I (12) _____ (try) to explain to them. I (13) _____ (tell) them that my friend's plane (14) _____ (land) ten minutes ago. But they (15) _____ not _____ (listen) to my excuse. I (16) _____ (have) to pay £50 the next day.

9.6 Past perfect: simple or continuous
(PBEG 25.4; 26.2; 40.1)

Use the verb in brackets and the past perfect in simple or continuous formation to complete the sentences below. In three of these sentences, both formations are possible.

Example: It was the most beautiful house I _____ ever _____ (see).
Answer: It was the most beautiful house I <u>had</u> ever <u>seen</u>.

1 I _____ (have) trouble with a front tooth for several days.
2 I _____ (have) trouble with that tooth before.
3 I explained that I _____ already _____ (have) lunch.
4 He _____ never _____ (work) in a factory before.
5 He _____ only _____ (work) there for a few days when he decided to leave.
6 I _____ (watch) the match on the Saturday before and I was looking forward to the next one.
7 The next match proved to be the most exciting one I _____ ever _____ (watch).
8 I _____ (watch) for nearly an hour when the TV screen suddenly went blank.

10
MODAL VERBS

Modal verbs are auxiliaries. They are always the first word in the verb of the sentence. But they are different from other auxiliaries; they never change their form. After a modal, the next verb is always base form.

NOTE For practice with modals in tag questions, look at Extra Exercises 3.

10.1 Word order (PBEG 27)

Change the order of the words or groups of words to make a correct sentence.
Example: should / you / have done / better than that
Answer: You should have done better than that.

1 told me / you / have / might
2 terrible / must / be feeling / he
3 have done that / not / you / should
4 how many days / be staying? / you / will
5 here six weeks / have been / I / will
6 helped you / have / would / she
7 must / have got / it / lost in the post
8 known / never have / would / I

10.2 The correct verb form (PBEG 27)

Fill in the gap with the correct form of the verb in brackets.
Example: I would _____ (have) _____ (meet) you if I'd known.
Answer: I would <u>have met</u> you if I'd known.

1 I can't _____ (tell) you now, but try again tomorrow.
2 You must _____ (do) it immediately.
3 While you're relaxing on holiday, I'll _____ (be) _____ (work) hard at the office.
4 They'll _____ (have) _____ (have) lunch by now.
5 I could _____ (have) _____ (do) that myself but you didn't ask.
6 You shouldn't _____ (have) _____ (be) _____ (drive) without lights.
7 You might _____ (have) _____ (have) an accident.
8 When should they _____ (be) _____ (arrive)?
9 When will you _____ (be) going to visit them?

10.3 Continuous formation (PBEG 27.1)

Fill in the gap with one of the verbs below and use the continuous formation.

have work help go get arrive leave stay

Example: When will you _____ for England?
Answer: When will you <u>be leaving</u> for England?

1 I may _____ to England next year.
2 Don't just sit there! You should _____ John with the work.
3 I really must _____ now, or I'll miss the last bus.
4 He'll _____ all afternoon and he can't see anyone.
5 It's nearly twelve and they haven't returned, so they must _____ a
   great time.
6 I should _____ on with this work or I'll never finish it.
7 How long will you _____ at the hotel?
8 I want to meet him at the airport. When will he _____?

10.4 Perfect simple formation (PBEG 27.1)

*Fill in the gap with one of the verbs below and use the perfect simple
formation.*

help tell be go win get do

Example: I could _____ you that myself.
Answer: I could <u>have told</u> you that myself.

1 You may _____ top of the class, but you're a lazy student.
2 I could never _____ this without you.
3 If they hadn't caught me, I wouldn't _____ sent to gaol.
4 You should _____ to the lesson yesterday.
5 You might _____ me, instead of just standing there.
6 But they can't _____ lost; it's easy to find the way.
7 John should _____ chosen to play. Then we might _____.

10.5 Perfect continuous formation (PBEG 27.1)

*Fill in the gap with one of the verbs below and use the perfect continuous
formation.*

sleep play teach have

Example: John ought to _____ for us. Then we would have won.
Answer: John ought to <u>have been playing</u> for us. Then we would have
        won.

1 By next month I will _____ at this school for six years.
2 They didn't answer the door. They must _____ when we called.
3 He might _____ lunch in the cafeteria.
4 Wouldn't he _____ football at that time?

10.6 *The correct verb formation* (PBEG 27)

Fill in the gap with the verb in brackets and use the correct verb formation.
Example: He arrived quickly. He must _____ (take) a taxi.
Answer: He arrived quickly. He must <u>have taken</u> a taxi.

1 If you want to learn the guitar, you must _____ (take) lessons.
2 Maria goes to music school. She must _____ (take) guitar lessons.
3 Maria can play the guitar! She couldn't last year. She must _____ (take) lessons.
4 I'm afraid I can't _____ (come) to the party tomorrow night.
5 He can't _____ (hear) the news. He's been away for six months.
6 You shouldn't _____ (walk) here in this weather. I could _____ (give) you a lift. Come in and get warm. You must _____ (freeze).

11

OTHER VERB CONSTRUCTIONS

There are some verbal constructions with the same kind of meaning as modals but their formation is not always the same. This section gives you practice in using them correctly.

NOTE For practice with these constructions in tag questions, look at Extra Exercises 3.

11.1 *Word order* (PBEG 34.1; 36; 37.1; 38)

Change the order of the words or groups of words to make a correct sentence.

Example: ought / you / to have done / better than that
Answer: You ought to have done better than that.

1 finish it / you / n't / need
2 to / you / be there by now / ought
3 have got / work late / to / I
4 finish it / I was not / to / able
5 better / I / talk to him / had
6 get a new job / to / am going / I
7 wear a uniform? / did you / to / have
8 never used / work so hard / we / to

11.2 *The correct verb form* (PBEG 34.1; 36–8)

*Fill in the gap with the correct form of the verb in brackets. Add **to** if it is necessary.*

Example: I was _____ (go) _____ (visit) you but you were out.
Answer: I was <u>going to visit</u> you but you were out.

1 We'll just have _____ (have) the meeting next week.
2 You _____ (have) better _____ (be) more careful next time.
3 What else have you _____ (get) _____ (do) today?
4 You don't _____ (need) _____ (spend) much money to live there.
5 He has not _____ (be) able _____ (walk) for several years now.
6 He _____ (use) _____ (go) out a lot but now he stays at home.
7 He is _____ (use) _____ (stay) at home.
8 I don't want to but I _____ (be) going _____ (have) _____ (talk) to her.

9 I _____ (use) _____ (be) able _____ (do) that, but I'm too old now.

10 I ought _____ (have) _____ (get) used _____ (work) indoors but I still find it difficult.

11 You _____ (need) n't _____ (go) there if you don't want to.

11.3 Need (PBEG 34; 35.3)

Fill in the gap with **need** *and use the correct verb formation. Add* **to** *if it is necessary. Be careful with negatives.*

Example: I _____ repair the car. It's working well.
Answer: I <u>don't need</u> to repair the car. It's working well.

1 It's OK. You _____ finish it if you don't want to.

2 You'll _____ buy a coat if you're going to Scotland. It's very cold there.

3 You'll _____ a coat in Scotland. It's very cold there.

4 You _____ sunglasses. It rains most of the time.

5 I _____ buy a new coat when I got to Scotland. It was so cold.

6 I _____ a new coat in Scotland. It was so cold.

7 I _____ have taken sunglasses. It rained all the time.

8 I _____ take my sunglasses out so I left them in the hotel.

11.4 Have to (PBEG 34)

Fill in the gap with **have to** *and use the correct verb formation. Be careful with negatives.*

Example: She _____ see the doctor every day this week.
Answer: She <u>has to</u> see the doctor every day this week.

1 I'm afraid I'll _____ work late tonight.

2 This work _____ be finished today. I'll be home late.

3 But I _____ work tomorrow morning. I can have a rest.

4 I _____ work late yesterday. There was extra work to do. It _____ be done as quickly as possible.

5 Don't do the homework now. It _____ be handed in until next week.

6 I _____ do any work yesterday. I had a rest.

7 He _____ never _____ do a day's work in his life.

11.5 Be going to (PBEG 37)

Fill in the gap with the correct form of **be going to** *and the words in brackets.*

Example: _____ (they go) to the beach, but it started to rain.
Answer: <u>They were going</u> to go to the beach, but it started to rain.

1 This traffic's terrible. ———— (I be) late again.

2 ———— (I not tell) you. I don't want to.

3 They say ———— (it be) a very bad winter.

4 When ———— (you buy) a new shirt?

5 I'm sorry, ———— (I tell) you but I forgot.

6 ———— (we just leave) the house when the phone rang.

7 ———— (you change) that light or shall I do it myself?

8 ———— (I not go) out today, but it looks like I must.

11.6 Used to (PBEG 38)

Fill in the gap with **used to** *and use the correct form of the words in brackets.*

Example: They ———— (live) in England before they came here.

Answer: They used to live in England before they came here.

1 I've known him for years. He ———— (live) next door to me.

2 We ———— (play) together when we were children.

3 He ———— (never be) such an unfriendly person.

4 He ———— (not work) so hard, did he?

5 He ———— (not get up) early in the morning.

6 I don't think he is ———— (get up) so early in the morning.

7 It took me a while to get ———— (get up) so early myself.

8 My mother ———— (get up) early every morning.

NOTE For more practice with **used to** and past tense verb formations, look at Extra Exercises 4.

11.7 The correct verb formation (PBEG 34.1; 36; 38.1)

Complete the sentence with the words in brackets and any other necessary words. Be careful with negatives.

Example: I ———— (going go) to England next year.

Answer: I am going to go to England next year.

1 He ———— (ought be) home by now.

2 He ———— (ought left) the office by now. It's very late.

3 I ———— (used work) at night, but then I changed to days.

4 You ———— (better clean) up that mess before I get back.

5 You ———— (need given) me that present. But thank you.

6 I ———— (better getting) on with this work.

7 I'm afraid I won't ———— (able come) to the party.

8 When I turned the key, the car wouldn't work. Luckily I ————
(able start) it with an old-fashioned starting handle.

12

MODAL MEANING AND USE

Sections 10 and 11 helped you practise the formation of modal verbs and other constructions. This section gives you practice in choosing which verb to use. Verbs with modal meaning say something about the speaker's or writer's feelings or thoughts. There are many different shades and types of feelings. For this reason, there is often more than one verb you can use in any one situation. Note also that the negative form of some of these verbs is not always the exact opposite of the affirmative.

12.1 Can *or* could (PBEG 28; 29)

Fill in the gap with **can** *or* **could**.
Example: When I was at school, I _____ never understand physics.
Answer: When I was at school, I <u>could</u> never understand physics.

1 Bees _____ fly, even though it seems impossible.
2 I _____ n't get to the shops today; they closed early.
3 He asked me if I _____ help with the washing, but I was too busy.
4 Take an umbrella. It _____ be raining when you get to England.
5 Take an umbrella. In England, it _____ rain at any time.
6 They say they _____ deliver it next week.
7 They said they _____ deliver it next week, but I told them not to.
8 You _____ leave the class when you've finished the exercise.

12.2 May *or* might (PBEG 30)

Fill in the gap with **may** *or* **might**.
Example: You _____ have told me. I came all this way for nothing.
Answer: You <u>might</u> have told me. I came all this way for nothing.

1 I thought he _____ be able to help me, but he was useless.
2 You _____ leave the class when you've finished the exercise.
3 I asked him if I _____ leave the class early.
4 Passengers _____ smoke at the back of the plane.

12.3 Can / could / might / be able to (PBEG 28–30)

Fill in the gap with **can, could, might** *or* **be able to**. *In some of these sentences, two answers are possible. Be careful with negatives.*
Example: Hurry! You _____ miss the bus.
Answer: Hurry! You <u>might</u> (or <u>could</u>) miss the bus.

1 _____ you help me lift this table? It's rather heavy.
2 I was wondering if I _____ use your phone.
3 Never mind! We _____ all make mistakes.
4 Some birds _____ fly a very long way.
5 There was a party last night but I _____ go.
6 She _____ n't have finished already!
7 I was lucky. I _____ get a taxi, so I arrived early.
8 I think you should arrive early or you _____ not get a seat.

12.4 Will / shall / would (PBEG 31; 32)

Fill in the gap with **will, shall** *or* **would**. *Use* **shall** *with only one of these sentences.*

Example: _____ you like some more coffee?
Answer: <u>Would</u> you like some more coffee?

1 Where _____ I put the ashtray?
2 Do you think we _____ get it done on time?
3 I wondered if we _____ get it done on time.
4 I _____ have a go if you like.
5 I _____ certainly like to have a go.
6 I _____ have had a go, but they didn't let me.
7 If we go tonight, it _____ be the third time I've seen that film.
8 I _____ have a green salad, please.
9 I _____ like a green salad, please.
10 He said he _____ have the salad, but he didn't eat any of it.
11 He just _____ eat anything these days. I don't know what to do.
12 Tell me, if you had a baby like this, what _____ you do?

12.5 Must *or* should (PBEG 33)

Fill in the gap with **must** *or* **should**.

Example: I don't think he _____ go to school today.
Answer: I don't think he <u>should</u> go to school today.

1 Have you got a toothache? I think you _____ go to the dentist.
2 Look at your teeth! You really _____ go to the dentist.
3 You think I'm going to buy that? You _____ be joking.
4 I was stupid to buy that ring. I _____ have realised it was a fake.
5 Why do you stay at home the whole time? You _____ be out having a good time.
6 It was a mistake to let in that goal. He _____ be feeling terrible right now.
7 I know I _____ n't have this cake, but I'm going to.

8 They _____ have got to the North Pole because they left the flag there.

12.6 *Probability and possibility* (PBEG 30.1; 33.3)

Fill in the gap with **should, shouldn't, must, can't** *or* **might**.
Example: After all that work, you _____ be tired.
Answer: After all that work, you <u>must</u> be tired.

1 You _____ find this exam difficult. The other exam was much harder.
2 They _____ have got lost, but I don't think so.
3 The robbers _____ have known where the money was. That's why they took everything so quickly.
4 Call the operator. She _____ be able to help you. That's her job.
5 Maria didn't say hello. But the room was very crowded. She _____ have seen me.
6 You'd better take an umbrella. It _____ rain.
7 I _____ be going to England, but I haven't decided yet.
8 There _____ be a mistake in this bill. The figures don't add up.

12.7 *Obligation – present and future time* (PBEG 33–5)

Fill in the gap with **must, should, have (got) to** *or* **need (to)**.
Sometimes more than one answer is possible. Be careful with negatives.
Example: In England, people with dogs _____ have a dog licence.
Answer: In England, people with dogs <u>have to</u> have a dog licence.
Example: But you _____ have a licence for a cat.
Answer: But you <u>don't have to</u> have a licence for a cat.

1 I _____ wear glasses when I read, but I don't.
2 I _____ wear glasses for reading, but I _____ wear them for anything else.
3 You _____ tell me. I already know.
4 You _____ never drive too fast.
5 You _____ drive so slowly; there's nothing else on the road.
6 Important notice: These doors _____ be kept locked at all times.
7 I _____ go to a meeting tomorrow. I hope it doesn't take long.
8 In my opinion, you _____ go to the lesson. I think you _____ study by yourself instead.
9 It's alright, you _____ come to the lesson. I won't mark you absent.
10 Passengers _____ not talk to the driver while the bus is moving. Penalty: £25.

12.8 Obligation – past time (PBEG 33–5)

Fill in the gap with the correct form of the verb in brackets and one of the forms from the list below.

had to   should have   shouldn't have   didn't need to
didn't have to   needn't have

Example: You _____ (tell) me. I already knew.
Answer: You <u>needn't have told</u> me. I already knew.

1   I _____ (see) the dentist yesterday. It was horrible.

2   Maria _____ (see) the dentist. She's very lucky.

Yesterday, I left my wallet in a shop and I (3) _____ (go) back for it. I was angry about this because I (4) _____ (go) out at all. I already had everything I needed at home. I walked back, thinking that I (5) _____ (be) more careful. I was afraid that I would never see my wallet again, but I (6) _____ (worry). The shopkeeper had it. He told me that I (7) _____ (be) so careless. I offered to give him a reward but he said that I (8) _____ (give) him anything; it was just part of his service.

12.9 *Will* or *be going to* (PBEG 31; 37.2)

*Fill in the gap with the correct form of **will** or **be going to**.*

Example: I _____ go to England next week. I'm very excited.
Answer: I <u>am going to</u> go to England next week. I'm very excited.

1   Can you help me? My car _____ start.

2   Yes, just wait a minute and then I _____ have a look for you.

3   It's easy to see that your car _____ start. You'd better get a bus.

4   Give me a hand with moving this desk, _____ you?

5   _____ you just _____ sit there like a vegetable all day?

6   I _____ pass that exam if it kills me.

7   I _____ believe that when I see it!

8   I _____ attend that lecture tomorrow. I've heard she's a very good speaker.

NOTE For more practice with verb formations and future time (**will, be going to**, present simple, present continuous), look at Extra Exercises 5.

13

PASSIVE

We make passive verb formations with the verb **be** before a past participle. In a passive sentence, something happens to the subject (the subject is not an agent). Passive is useful when the agent is obvious, or not important, or is 'new' information, and also when the speaker/writer does not want to be rude.

13.1 Understanding (PBEG 42)

Answer the following questions with 'Yes', 'No' or 'We don't know'.

John was liked by all his classmates.

1 Did John like his classmates?
2 Did John's classmates like him?

John thought he was going to be hit by the ball.

3 Did John think that / he would hit the ball?
4 Did John think that / the ball would hit him?

13.2 Word order (PBEG 42; 43)

Change the order of words or groups of words to make a correct sentence.
Example: the other students / she was / by / helped
Answer: She was helped by the other students.

1 a decision / taken yet? / been / has
2 told / can / now the truth / be
3 told / they had not / about the meeting / been
4 told / my grandfather / by / I was
5 be / where will / the 1996 Olympic Games / held?
6 by / arrested / he was / the police
7 given / the Nobel Prize / he / has been
8 to be / seen / has / to be believed / this machine

13.3 The correct form of **be** (PBEG 43)

*Fill in the gap with **am, is, are, was, were, be, been** or **being**.*
Example: She has not _____ told yet.
Answer: She has not <u>been</u> told yet.

1 William the Conqueror _____ crowned King of England in 1066.
2 Communication lines have _____ cut by the storm.

3 The buses in London used to _____ controlled by the Council.
4 Could I use your washing machine? Mine is _____ repaired.
5 They _____ last seen getting on a plane at the London airport.
6 Children should _____ seen and not heard.
7 Don't count your chickens before they _____ hatched.
8 If you arrive late, you will not _____ allowed to enter.

13.4 The correct verb formation (PBEG 43)

Fill in the gap with the correct formation of the verb in brackets.
Example: When we arrived, the floor _____ (cover) in dirt.
Answer: When we arrived, the floor <u>was covered</u> in dirt.

1 You _____ (advise) to remain seated at all times.
2 Bags should not _____ (leave) alone at any time.
3 Carpets _____ (make) here for centuries.
4 This film _____ (produce) by Steven Spielberg in 1979.
5 In the past, ice had _____ (buy) from the iceman.
6 Refreshments will _____ (provide) in the interval.
7 The flight from Rome _____ (delay) by fog. It is arriving late.
8 The news that the President _____ (shoot) travelled around the world.

NOTE For more practice with the difference between active and passive verb formations after **be**, look at Extra Exercises 6.

13.5 Active to passive (PBEG 42–4)

Change these active sentences into passive. Remember that it is often better not to mention the agent in a passive sentence.
Example: The news had not worried John at first. (active)
Answer: John had not been worried by the news at first. (passive)

1 How do you spell that, please?
2 Finally, an old school friend recognised him.
3 Everybody expected him to win the race.
4 I'm sorry, but we just can't do it.
5 The earthquake killed my grandmother.
6 They have closed down that old hotel.
7 You can see the top of the building from thirty kilometres away.
8 They must have told her about it.
9 Has anybody seen him in the last few days?
10 Why didn't you tell me about this before?
11 Don't worry! Nobody will see us from here.
12 I arrived to find that they had stopped the game because of the weather.

13.6 *Active or passive* (PBEG 42–4)

Look at each active sentence below.

a Can we give the same meaning in a passive sentence?

If yes, b Is it better to use passive?

If yes, c Change the sentence to passive.

Example: My father works extremely hard.

Answer: We cannot use passive here. (the agent is 'my father' and there is no other possible subject)

Example: Maria drives a Toyota.

Answer: We can use passive but it is better to use active here. (the 'Toyota' is new information)

1   Everybody knows him well.
2   We think she will have the baby next week.
3   A cat has nine lives.
4   John has bought an expensive new car.
5   A tall dark stranger has bought my car.
6   I feel terrible.
7   Help! An insect has bitten me on the leg.
8   I could have danced all night.
9   Look at these batteries! Somebody should have replaced them ages ago.
10 We got a beautiful view from the top of the tower.
11 We are sorry to inform you that we have not selected you for the job.
12 Who spilt all this milk?
13 Penguin publishes this book.
14 I need a new pair of shoes.
15 Fantastic news! The British Council has given me a scholarship.
16 Maria refuses to meet John at the airport.

14

NOUNS AND NOUN PHRASES

English nouns have very few forms. Some of them have four forms but many important nouns have only one or two forms. Some unit nouns do not have a genitive form – they use **of** instead. Most mass nouns and verbal nouns do not have a genitive form or a plural form.

NOTE For more practice with choosing the correct verb form for the subject (singular or plural), look at Extra Exercises 7.

14.1 Counting and plurals (PBEG 46; 47)

Complete the sentence with the correct form of the word in brackets. Use any other necessary words. Sometimes more than one answer is possible.

Example: He ate three _____ (cheese).
Answer: He ate three <u>pieces of</u> cheese.
Example: We had six _____ (lesson).
Answer: We had six <u>lessons</u>.

1 Many small _____ (village) were destroyed.
2 I've got three _____ (homework) to do this evening.
3 Lots of _____ (person) were unhappy about it.
4 There were two important _____ (news).
5 Why are there three _____ (pyjamas)?
6 Several _____ (child) got lost on the way to school.
7 I'd like five _____ (rice), please.
8 I've got only two _____ (luggage).
9 There were four serious car _____ (crash) this weekend.
10 He can give you lots of important _____ (information).
11 It was autumn, and the _____ (leaf) were falling.
12 There is a lot of _____ (pollution) in this town.
13 Some _____ (family) celebrate Christmas on December 24th.
14 We've got three _____ (fish) for dinner.
15 How many _____ (toast) do you want?
16 Can I have a few _____ (paper) to write on?
17 Three _____ (policeman) came round.
18 Let me give you a few _____ (advice).
19 You need about six and a half _____ (material) to make those curtains.

20   I was so thirsty I drank four _____ (water) one after the other.

21   He's only five _____ (month) old and he's already got two
_____ (tooth).

22   There are eleven _____ (furniture) in the room, including three
_____ (desk).

14.2   *Proper nouns*   (PBEG 48.1; appendix 2)

*The passage below is badly written. Rewrite it, using capital letters in the
correct places and the word 'the' in the two places where it is missing.*

Example: london stands on river thames
Answer: London stands on the river Thames.

margaret thatcher grew up in grantham, a small town in lincolnshire in
north of england. she became a member of parliament in the 1950s and
became leader of the conservative party in 1977. she became prime
minister of the united kingdom of great britain and northern ireland after
the general election of 1979. like all elections in britain, it was held on a
thursday. she is the first woman leader of a large industrialised nation in
europe. like all the prime ministers before her, she went to live in 10
downing street. downing street is in london, close to houses of
parliament.

14.3   *Verbal nouns*   (PBEG 48.2)

*Fill in the gap with the verb in brackets and use the **-ing** form or **to** + base
form.*

Example: I'd like _____ (see) you tomorrow.
Answer: I'd like <u>to see</u> you tomorrow.
Example: I like _____ (watch) comedies.
Answer: I like <u>watching</u> comedies.

I don't really enjoy (**1**) _____ (travel) by plane. On a plane last week, I
noticed two men in front of me (**2**) _____ (smoke), although there
were signs telling passengers not (**3**) _____ (smoke). I don't like
people (**4**) _____ (smoke) near me, so I went (**5**) _____ (remind)
them that (**6**) _____ (smoke) was not allowed. I asked if they would
mind (**7**) _____ (put) out their cigarettes. When they saw me they
both stopped (**8**) _____ (talk) and turned round (**9**) _____ (look) at
me. When I asked again, they refused. Instead of (**10**) _____
(apologise), they kept on (**11**) _____ (smoke) and started (**12**) _____
(argue) with me. The other passengers started (**13**) _____ (look) at us
and I felt very embarrassed. Only one of them did all the (**14**) _____
(talk). I remember the other one just (**15**) _____ (sit) there and
(**16**) _____ (blow) smoke in my face. I am not used to (**17**) _____
(be) insulted and I felt like (**18**) _____ (punch) him on the nose.

Fortunately, I managed (**19**) _____ (stop) myself from (**20**) _____ (do) this.

14.4   *The correct noun form*   (PBEG 46; 49)

Fill in the gap with the correct form of the word in brackets.

Example: Hello. I'm _____ (Maria) husband.

Answer: Hello. I'm <u>Maria's</u> husband.

1   He doesn't like _____ (woman) drivers because they are so slow.

2   He doesn't believe in _____ (woman) rights.

3   He thinks that a _____ (woman) place is in the home.

4   He said all this to a _____ (woman) doctor.

5   She didn't like these old-fashioned _____ (belief).

6   She said he was one of the rudest _____ (man) she had ever met.

7   She thought _____ (person) like him should keep quiet.

8   She thought he had _____ (family) problems.

9   Do you have a _____ (child) with long brown hair?

10   Is there a _____ (child) playground here?

11   Is there a place for _____ (child) here?

12   I went to _____ (Maria) school yesterday.

13   I went to the _____ (music) school yesterday.

14   Where's my _____ (shopping) bag?

15   There is a _____ (clothes) shop over there.

16   My _____ (office) desk has gone.

14.5   *Genitive noun phrases*   (PBEG 49)

Complete the sentence with a noun phrase which means the same as the sentence above it.

Example: Maria has a father.

Answer: He's <u>Maria's father</u>.

Example: The match has ended.

Answer: It's the <u>end of the match</u>.

Example: This school teaches music.

Answer: It's a <u>music school</u>.

1   Children play in this playground.

It's a _____.

2   England has a capital.

London is the _____.

3 London has a mayor.

He is the _____.

4 This car has five doors.

It's a _____.

5 I have some friends. I met one.

I met a _____.

6 There is a hospital in the town.

It's the _____.

7 The Director has a secretary.

She's the _____.

8 The people chose him.

He was the _____.

9 The university has a car park.

It's the _____.

10 This is the world of tomorrow.

It's _____.

11 My cousin has friends.

They are _____.

12 My cousins have one daughter.

She is _____.

13 They teach languages at this school.

It's a _____.

14 It's a card for phones.

It's a _____.

15 You use cards for this phone.

It's a _____.

16 You can use this machine to make coffee.

It's a _____.

17 Maria has a fiancé.

   He's _____.

18 A baker has a shop.

   It's a _____.

19 This shop sells clothes.

   It's a _____.

20 This is a battery for cars.

   It's a _____.

NOTE For practice with apostrophe **s** (**'s**) (genitive or **is** or **has**), look at Extra Exercises 1.

15

PRONOUNS

If the reader or listener already knows what we are talking about, we do not need to use a long noun phrase; we can use a pronoun instead.

15.1 Personal pronouns (PBEG 50)

Fill in the gap with the correct personal pronoun.

Example: Have the children taken _____ coats with _____?
Answer: Have the children taken <u>their</u> coats with <u>them</u>?

1 Hey, come back! That's _____ bicycle you're taking.
2 Hey, come back! That bicycle is _____ and I need it.
3 _____ have to listen carefully or you might misunderstand him.
4 _____ are going to build the new road through our village; we'll have to move.
5 I wished _____ a safe journey as he left.
6 Look after _____! Don't do anything silly.
7 There are five of _____, so we can't all fit in one car.
8 We were terrified by the noise. But _____ was only John trying to play the saxophone.
9 I had already lost my key, and then Maria lost _____! We were locked out.
10 John can't play tomorrow; he's broken _____ ankle.
11 You can walk there if you like but _____ will take you an hour.
12 What a clever child! She's done it all by _____.
13 The school had problems and nobody knew what to do about _____.
14 _____ was three o'clock before we left.
15 Have you heard the news? _____ say Queen Elizabeth is coming to visit!
16 They introduced me to John. He's a friend of _____.
17 I'm not going to help you. _____ must do it _____.
18 I wonder if you could help _____. We're lost.
19 Do you think _____ will rain today?

I've got (20) _____ tickets and we're flying to London tomorrow. I talked to the others and (21) _____ are all excited about it. I think (22) _____ is very exciting (23) _____.

NOTE For practice with the difference between **they're, their** and **there**, look at Extra Exercises 8.

15.2 Relative pronouns (PBEG 60)

*Fill in the gap with **who, which, where** or **whose** or if possible leave it blank.*
Example: That's the car _____ was in the accident.
Answer: That's the car <u>which</u> was in the accident.

1 People _____ drink and drive often go to prison.
2 He's the man _____ daughter won the competition.
3 I want to go to a place _____ the sun always shines.
4 The man _____ I saw wasn't the Director.
5 Pollution is a problem _____ just won't go away.
6 There were some children _____ playing in the park.
7 Borstal is a place _____ children _____ have broken the law are sent.

15.3 **That** as a relative pronoun

*Do 15.2 again, but this time use **that** whenever it is possible.*

15.4 Personal pronouns or relative pronouns
(PBEG 50;60)

Fill in the gap with the correct pronoun.
Example: People _____ live in glass houses shouldn't throw stones.
Answer: People <u>who</u> (<u>that</u>) live in glass houses shouldn't throw stones.

1 Those are the people _____ live next door.
2 Those are the people! _____ live next door.
3 Maria is the only one _____ passed the exam.
4 Anyone _____ has finished can go.
5 Borstal is a place that children _____ have broken the law are sent to.
6 These are the children _____ were lost.
7 These are the children. _____ mother is worried about them.
8 These are the children _____ mother is worried about them.

15.5 Third person pronouns (PBEG 50; 59)

*Fill in the gap with **one, ones, it, they** or **them**.*
Example: I'm having prawns. _____ taste lovely. Here, try _____.
Answer: I'm having prawns. <u>They</u> taste lovely. Here, try <u>one</u>.

1 If you don't like the red coat, take the blue _____.
2 I don't need the coat. Take _____ if you want.
3 I needed a pen so I asked to borrow _____.
4 I needed his pen so I asked to borrow _____.

5 I couldn't get a good seat. The best _____ were all taken.
6 I couldn't get a seat. _____ were all taken.
7 I couldn't get a good seat. The best of _____ were all taken.
8 I see you're making coffee. Could you make me _____ too?
9 I need those boxes over there? Could you pass me _____?
10 No, not that box, the other _____!
11 I see you're having snails for lunch. I've never had _____. Could I just try _____?

16

DETERMINERS: THE ARTICLES

This section and the next section give you practice with using words which go before a noun. The words we can use (or not use) can depend on whether the noun is singular or plural or mass but they can also depend on other things.

16.1 A / an / some / any (PBEG 51)

Fill in the gap with **a, an, some** *or* **any.**
Example: I'd like _____ information, please.
Answer: I'd like <u>some</u> information, please.

1 Give her _____ chance!
2 I had _____ opportunity but I missed it.
3 It was _____ very good opportunity.
4 I don't think I will get _____ more opportunities.
5 I don't think I will get _____ chance like that again.
6 I didn't get _____ money for it.
7 Still, it was _____ useful lesson.
8 It was _____ unusual experience.
9 I learnt _____ useful lessons from it.
10 My friends gave me _____ good advice.
11 Didn't you buy _____ apples?
12 When I saw him, he gave me _____ money.

16.2 Some / any *with* one, body, thing, *and* where (PBEG 5.4; 51)

Fill in the gap with one word from the list below.
something anything somewhere anywhere someone / somebody anyone / anybody
Example: I think there's _____ at the door.
Answer: I think there's <u>someone</u> at the door. (or **somebody**)

1 Let me tell you _____.
2 I went to school but there wasn't _____ there.
3 All the other students had gone _____.
4 I couldn't find them _____.
5 I couldn't think of _____ to do.

6 Has _____ seen my pullover?

7 There is _____ strange going on here.

8 _____ must meet Maria at the station.

16.3 A / an / some / any *alone or in compounds*
(PBEG 5.4; 51)

Fill in the gap with one word from the list below.

a an some any something anything somewhere anywhere someone / somebody anyone / anybody

Example: We didn't go _____ last night.

Answer: We didn't go <u>anywhere</u> last night.

1 I can't find _____ to write with.

2 There aren't _____ pens in the store room.

3 _____ wants you on the phone.

4 There are _____ people to see you.

5 You're not going _____ until you finish your dinner.

6 My hair is terrible. I can't do _____ thing with it.

7 It's not worth doing _____ with my hair. It always looks bad.

8 There must be a decent bookshop _____ in this town.

16.4 A / an / some / any *or the* (PBEG 51; 52; 54)

Fill in the gap with a, an, some, any or the.

Example: She was _____ best student in our class.

Answer: She was <u>the</u> best student in our class.

1 This is _____ last time I'm ever going to _____ film with you.

2 I went to _____ post office in Church Street to buy _____ stamps.

3 Where did you learn to play _____ saxophone like that?
I learnt it from _____ private teacher.

4 We told _____ children that they would not get _____ presents if they behaved badly.

5 I see _____ postman has come. Are there _____ letters for me today?

6 It is hard to find _____ good husband these days.

7 Well, I think I've got _____ nicest husband in _____ world.

We had (**8**) _____ wonderful time on our holiday. (**9**) _____ beaches were clean and (**10**) _____ people were very friendly.

(**11**) _____ few people still live in (**12**) _____ centre of (**13**) _____ city but rents are more than £150 (**14**) _____ week so most people can't afford it.

16.5 A / an / some / any or zero (PBEG 51; 53; 54)

*Fill in the gap with **a, an, some** or **any** or leave it blank.*

Example: What's that? It's _____ salt.
Answer: What's that? It's salt. (leave it blank)

1 He told us he was _____ student.
2 They told us they were _____ students.
3 _____ good quality meat is difficult to get round here.
4 That's _____ great news. Congratulations!
5 Could I have _____ sugar, please?
6 What! I didn't know you took _____ sugar in your tea.
7 Yes, they sell _____ fruit at that shop but they didn't have _____
   oranges left when I got there.

16.6 *The* or zero (PBEG 48.1; 52–4)

*Fill in the gap with **the** or leave it blank.*

Example: I like _____ Maria.
Answer: I like Maria. (leave it blank)

1 I don't like _____ people who don't like me.
2 All _____ people of _____ town were very excited.
3 Vegetarians are _____ people who don't eat _____ meat.
4 We all went by _____ car but Maria took _____ eight o'clock
   train instead.
5 We got back to _____ house at ten o'clock and went straight to
   _____ bed.

I'm afraid (**6**) _____ Maria isn't here. She's at (**7**) _____ work now
and after that she's going to (**8**) _____ bank.

Most (**9**) _____ people do not like working at (**10**) _____ night.
They prefer to work during (**11**) _____ day.

(**12**) _____ fuel that (**13**) _____ cars use is called (**14**) _____
petrol in (**15**) _____ Britain, but in (**16**) _____ America they call it
(**17**) _____ gas.

I come from (**18**) _____ United Kingdom of (**19**) _____ Great
Britain and (**20**) _____ Northern Ireland. That's (**21**) _____ official
name of (**22**) _____ country, but there are other names for it.
Sometimes it's called (**23**) _____ United Kingdom in (**24**) _____
official publications. Other people call it (**25**) _____ Great Britain, or
GB for short; that's what you can see on (**26**) _____ back of
(**27**) _____ cars. (**28**) _____ simplest name is just (**29**) _____

Britain. You should not call (**30**) _____ country (**31**) _____ England because this makes people from (**32**) _____ Scotland, (**33**) _____ Wales and (**34**) _____ Northern Ireland very angry. (**35**) _____ Scotland is where I live now. I live in (**36**) _____ Highlands. These are in (**37**) _____ northern part of this country.

16.7 *The correct article* (PBEG 51–4)

Fill in the gap with **a, an, some, any** *or* **the** *or leave it blank.*
Example: Could you tell me _____ time, please?
Answer: Could you tell me <u>the</u> time, please?

She's (**1**) _____ friend from (**2**) _____ school. In fact, she's (**3**) _____ best friend I have from there.

We usually have (**4**) _____ dinner at about eight, but yesterday we had (**5**) _____ early dinner and then we went to (**6**) _____ cinema.

(**7**) _____ Johnsons were (**8**) _____ family of (**9**) _____ farmers. They lived next to (**10**) _____ River Erewash.

(**11**) _____ leader of (**12**) _____ United Nations Organization is called (**13**) _____ Secretary General. (**14**) _____ United Nations usually meets in (**15**) _____ New York in (**16**) _____ USA.

Four hundred years ago, (**17**) _____ number of (**18**) _____ English speakers in (**19**) _____ world was about six million. Now about 300 million people speak (**20**) _____ English as their mother-tongue, and another 100 million use it as (**21**) _____ second language.

I had my first baby in (**22**) _____ hospital. She was born in (**23**) _____ morning on (**24**) _____ third of December. But I didn't like (**25**) _____ doctors and nurses at (**26**) _____ hospital so I had my second baby at (**27**) _____ home.

It was (**28**) _____ beautiful day. (**29**) _____ sky was blue and (**30**) _____ sun was shining. We had gone for (**31**) _____ walk by (**32**) _____ sea. Everything was quiet; we were (**33**) _____ only people there. Suddenly, we saw (**34**) _____ people walking towards us. We didn't know them but when they got closer, we saw that they were (**35**) _____ fishermen.

17

OTHER DETERMINERS

This section gives you more practice with words which go before a noun. The words we can use (or not use) can depend on whether the noun is singular or plural or mass, but they can also depend on other things.

NOTE For practice with choosing the correct verb form for the subject (singular or plural), look at Extra Exercises 7.

17.1 This / that / these / those (PBEG 55)

Fill in the gap with **this, that, these** *or* **those**.

Example: Can you pass me _____ pen over there?
Answer: Can you pass me <u>that</u> pen over there?

1 Alright, I'll do it, but _____ is the last time.
2 Do you know _____ people who live next door?
3 I'm glad _____'s finished.
4 What shall I do with _____ plates here?
5 _____ was one of the worst films I've ever seen.
6 Hello, _____ is John. How are you?
7 Who was _____ on the phone?
8 _____ is bad luck. I hope you have better luck next time.
9 _____ is a bit worrying, I can't find my wallet.
10 Can you see _____ bridge? The bank is just on the other side of it.
11 Feel _____ material. Lovely, isn't it?
12 _____ weather is getting on my nerves.
13 I was walking to work when I saw _____ man asleep by the side of the road.
14 Pollution is getting worse and worse. _____ is a major problem.
15 John, I'd like you to meet someone. _____ is Maria. She'll introduce you to _____ people you want to meet.

17.2 Many / much / a lot (of) / lots (of)
(PBEG 56; 57.1)

Fill in the gap with **many, much, a lot / lots** *or* **a lot of / lots of**.

Example: There was _____ coffee in the jar.
Answer: There was <u>a lot of</u> coffee in the jar. (or <u>lots of</u>)

1 How _____ petrol do we need?

2 How _____ litres of petrol do we need?

3 How _____ teeth has he got now?

4 There is too _____ noise in here.

5 _____ people come here for the healthy air.

6 Hurry up! We haven't got _____ time left.

7 We've got _____ time before the plane comes. Let's go and have some coffee.

8 How _____ times have you been to England?

9 Do you have _____ friends there?

10 We need money for the bus. How _____ have we got?

11 John's got _____ money. Let's ask him for some.

12 You should have seen how _____ he ate! I couldn't believe it.

13 I've got so _____ to do, I don't know where to start.

14 I've got _____ to do today, so I'd better get an early start.

15 He talked _____ but nobody else said very _____.

17.3 *A few or a little* (PBEG 56)

*Fill in the gap with **a few** or **a little**.*

Example: There were already _____ people waiting at the gate.
Answer: There were already <u>a few</u> people waiting at the gate.

1 Hurry up! We've only got _____ minutes left.

2 Hurry up! We've only got _____ time left.

3 Now add _____ water.

4 Now add _____ drops of water.

5 I get by with _____ help from my friends.

6 We were all there but only _____ of us saw what really happened.

7 Could I have _____ more soup, please?

8 _____ loving goes a long way.

17.4 *Of after determiners* (PBEG 57)

*Fill in the gap with **of** or leave it blank.*

Example: Some _____ people are afraid of heights.
Answer: Some people are afraid of heights. (leave it blank)

1 Most _____ our teachers do not like marking homework.

2 Most _____ teachers do not like marking homework.

3 Most _____ us do not like marking homework.

4 Most _____ do not like marking homework.

5 None _____ the teachers here like marking essays.

6 No _____ teachers here like marking essays.

7   I didn't see any _____ the students here.

8   I didn't see any _____ students here.

17.5 No / none / some / any *alone or in compounds*
(PBEG 51; 57)

Fill in the gap with one word from the list below.

**no   none   any   some   nobody   somebody   anybody   nothing
something   anything   nowhere   somewhere   anywhere**

Example: _____ was there; the place was empty.
Answer: <u>Nobody</u> was there; the place was empty.

1   What are we going to do? There isn't _____ food left.

2   What are we going to do? There is _____ food left.

3   We wanted some food but there was _____ left.

4   We wanted some food but _____ of it was left.

5   _____ of the food was good but the rest was terrible.

6   There's _____ place like home.

7   There's _____ like home.

8   He's won a million pounds? _____ people have all the luck!

9   _____ likes going to the dentist.

10 Never mind! Accidents can happen to _____.

11 _____ should have helped you. Then you would have been alright.

12 _____ in the world is safe from pollution these days.

13 I think it's best to say _____ about it. _____ things should be kept secret.

14 I wish _____ would help us. It doesn't matter who it is – _____ would do.

17.6 All *or* every (PBEG 57)

Fill in the gap with **all, every, everybody** *or* **everything**.

Example: I've read _____ the books he's written.
Answer: I've read <u>all</u> the book she's written.

1   We're having a sale and we're closing the shop. _____ must go.

2   _____ things must die.

3   Not _____ birds can fly.

4   Not _____ bird can fly.

5   _____ student passed the exam.

6   _____ the students passed the exam.

7   _____ of the students passed the exam.

8   _____ one of the students passed the exam.

17.7 Every or any *alone or in compounds* (PBEG 57)

Fill in the gap with one word from the list below.

every any everyone anyone everything anything everywhere anywhere

Example: He didn't tell _____; it was a complete secret.
Answer: He didn't tell <u>anyone</u>; it was a complete secret.

1 It's a stupid idea. Ask _____ and they'll tell you the same.
2 You don't know when you were born? I thought _____ knew that.
3 _____ time I come here, it rains.
4 You can see me _____ time you want to.
5 If _____ comes in, ask them to come back in half an hour.
6 Don't make so much noise; _____ is looking at us.
7 _____ he went, people wanted to talk to him.
8 We can go _____ you like. It's the same to me.
9 Please try to remember. _____ you can tell us might help.
10 I want you to tell me _____ that happened.
11 I'm cold and hungry. I'd do _____ for a good hot meal.
12 I trust him completely; I'll believe _____ he tells me.

17.8 Both / either / neither (PBEG 58)

Fill in the gap with **both, either** *or* **neither**.

Example: _____ of them knew. We had to ask somebody else.
Answer: <u>Neither</u> of them knew. We had to ask somebody else.

1 Cars may be parked on _____ sides of the road.
2 Cars may be parked on _____ side of the road.
3 Cars may be parked on _____ side; it's against the law.
4 Cars may not be parked on _____ side; it's against the law.
5 You can't park on _____ sides of the road at the same time; it's impossible.
6 _____ one of you knows what it's like to be poor.
7 You can take _____ bus; they _____ go to the town square.

17.9 A / an or one (PBEG 51; 59)

Fill in the gap with **a, an** *or* **one**.

Example: I had only _____ chance to pass the exam.
Answer: I had only <u>one</u> chance to pass the exam.

1 There's some cake left; would you like _____ piece?
2 There's only _____ piece left; all the others have been eaten.
3 Could I have _____ cigarette?

4 Don't tell her; she can't keep _____ secret for more than _____ few minutes.

5 This isn't _____ difficult exercise.

6 I've got just _____ more question left to do.

7 _____ way or another, I'm going to get there.

18

SENTENCES AND CLAUSES

This section gives you practice at making different types of sentences. Different verbs need different types of words to follow them. A sentence has only one main subject and one main verb, but sometimes there is another sentence inside the sentence. This is called a clause.

18.1 Word order (PBEG 60–63)

Change the order of the words or groups of words to make a correct sentence.
Example: have gone / where / I don't know / they
Answer: I don't know where they have gone.

1 is that / that / the car / the accident? / caused
2 he / the truth? / is telling / do you think
3 me / you / a question / ask / let
4 your coffee / you / I know / prefer / black
5 him / I am surprised / money / that / you lent
6 I don't know / knows / about it yet / he / if
7 in their / there / they think / office / a thief / is
8 that / that / that / I'm sure / hit me / is the man

18.2 Relative clauses (PBEG 60)

Complete the sentence so that it means the same as the sentence(s) above it.
Example: I know a man. He played football for England.
Answer: I know <u>a man who played football for England.</u>
Example: I know the man. He played football for England.
Answer: The man <u>I know played football for England.</u>
          (the relative pronoun **who** is not necessary)

1 A greengrocer sells fruit and vegetables.

   A greengrocer is a _____.

2 That supermarket stays open late.

   That's _____.

3 I know a place. Beautiful wild flowers grow there.

   I know _____.

4 I know the man. That's him over there.

   That's the _____.

5   His songs are popular all over the world. He's a pop star.

He is a pop star _____.

6   I saw a very helpful policeman.

The policeman _____.

7   The Lapps live in the far north of Scandinavia.

The Lapps are _____.

8   The family live next door. I met them.

I met _____.

9   I met the family. They live next door.

The family _____.

10 I saw a policeman. He was taking notes.

The policeman _____.

11 A policeman was taking notes. I saw him.

I saw _____.

12 People worry about pollution. It is a problem.

Pollution is _____.

13 Pollution is the big problem. People worry about it.

The big problem _____.

14 I only know one book on this subject. It is written by J. R. Smith.

The only _____.

15 I would like to live in a place. There is no pollution there.

I would _____.

16 Someone had found a photograph on the street. This was it.

It was a _____.

18.3 Empty subjects (PBEG 61)

Complete the sentence, beginning with It or There, so that it means the same as the sentence above it.

Example: Seeing you is nice.
Answer: It is nice to see you.
Example: A man is at the door.
Answer: There is a man at the door.

1 Talking to the driver is forbidden.

_____ driver.

2 This town has four bookshops.

_____ in _____.

3 In December 1988, a terrible earthquake happened in Armenia.

In December 1988, _____ was _____.

4 Losing your keys is horrible.

_____ keys.

5 The building fell down for several reasons.

_____ why _____.

6 Only five cars were left.

_____ left.

7 A strange man was at the window.

_____ window.

8 The person at the window was Maria.

_____ window.

9 We must go now.

_____ time _____.

10 We have a lot to do today.

_____ for us _____.

11 I last saw her five years ago.

_____ since I _____.

12 I still don't know a lot.

_____ that I don't know.

NOTE For practice with the difference between **there, their** and **they're,** look at Extra Exercises 8.

18.4 *The correct verb* (PBEG 62; 63)

Fill in the gap with one verb from the list below.

advise allow forgotten left let stop suggest wonder

Example: I _____ to take my umbrella.
Answer: I <u>forgot</u> to take my umbrella.

1 You look ill. I _____ that you see a doctor.
2 I _____ you to go to Dr Smith. He's very good.
3 The doctor won't _____ me get out of bed.
4 The doctor won't _____ me to get out of bed.
5 They took the money but I managed to _____ them taking the jewels.
6 I _____ if you could help me.
7 I've _____ my bag on the bus. I hope I can get it back.
8 I've _____ my bag again. I'll have to go home and get it.

18.5 *The correct verb form* (PBEG 62; 63)

Fill in the gap with the correct form of the verb in brackets. Use the word **to** *before the verb when it is necessary.*

Example: I want _____ (go).
Answer: I want <u>to go</u>.

1 They _____ (be) surprised that I had got the job.
2 He just left me _____ (stand) there.
3 It was very exciting _____ (see) him in real life.
4 We're having a language laboratory _____ (install) at our school.
5 The teacher made us _____ (stay) until we had finished.
6 He got lots of people _____ (help) him so it didn't take long.
7 I am pleased _____ (meet) you.
8 Politely but firmly, they asked us _____ (leave).

18.6 *Noun phrase + verb* (PBEG 63)

Complete each sentence so that it means the same as the sentence just above it.
Example: Everybody thinks that Argentina will win.
Answer: Everybody expects Argentina to win.

1 He was doing his homework when we found him.

   We found _____.

2 Somebody must wash those windows.

   I want those _____.

3 You must look after her.

   I want _____.

4 We were working until half past six before the teacher let us go.

   The teacher kept _____.

5 Some people cleaned the carpet for us.

   We had _____.

6 The robbers shot him; I saw them.

   I saw the _____.

7 He was lying by the roadside when they left him.

   They left _____.

8 They want to go, so why don't you let them?

   Why don't _____.

18.7 *Clauses with **that** / **if** / **whether** + question words* (PBEG 13; 63)

Complete each sentence so that it means the same as the sentences just above it.
Example: The weather would be fine. That's what the forecast said.
Answer: The forecast said (that) the weather would be fine.
        (**that** is not necessary, especially in speaking)

1 We had passed. That's what the teacher said.

   The teacher told _____.

2 'You have passed,' the teacher told us.

   The teacher told _____.

3 We have passed. The teacher has told us.

The teacher has _____.

4 He was going to jump. I was certain of that.

I was _____.

5 Perhaps the plane has landed. We'd better find out.

We'd better _____.

6 He likes that programme so much. I can't understand it.

I can't _____.

7 'Have you seen Maria?' That's what I asked him.

I asked _____.

8 Should I tell them about it or not? I just didn't know.

I just _____.

9 'Why are you late?' the teacher asked us.

The teacher wanted to _____.

10 'I'll be home by ten,' he said. But it's half past already!

He said he _____ but it's half past already.

11 It's a stupid idea. John thinks it's stupid too.

John agrees _____.

12 'What do you do for a living?' he asked.

He asked me _____.

18.8 *The correct meaning* (PBEG 62; 63)

Complete each sentence so that it means the same as the sentence just above it.
Example: The teacher let me leave early.
Answer: The teacher allowed <u>me to leave early</u>.

1 We hope you have a very happy birthday.

We wish _____.

2 He said that I was a liar.

He called _____.

3 You look silly in that hat.

That hat makes _____.

4 She was the boys' geography teacher last year.

She taught _____.

5 When they laughed at him, he became angry.

Their laughter _____.

6 Why don't you try another doctor?

I think you _____.

7 There must be another way to do this.

I'm sure _____.

8 Could I borrow £20 from you?

Could you _____.

19

ADJECTIVES, ADVERBS AND COMPARISON

Adjectives tell us something about a noun. Adverbs can give us information about any other part of a sentence, or even a whole sentence. The position of these two kinds of words in a sentence is important. We can make many adjectives into adverbs by adding **-ly**. We can also use adjectives and adverbs when we want to compare things. When we do this, many of them have special forms.

19.1 Word order (PBEG 64–7; 69; 70)

Change the order of the words or groups of words to make a correct sentence.
Example: Mercedes / big / he drives a / black
Answer: He drives a big black Mercedes.

1   very / he / fast / can run
2   a very / he / fast / is / runner
3   bottles on the shelf / green / ten / there were / big
4   he is / science / our / teacher / new
5   nice / TV is / very / new / our
6   seems / teacher / the / friendly / English
7   recorder / beautiful / it was a / cassette
8   stadium was / football / expensive / new / the
9   pool / new / swimming / Olympic / they've built a
10   processor / this is my / Amstrad / new / word
11   too / much / expensive / it is / for us
12   enough / big / for us to fit in / it isn't
13   just / there was / food / enough
14   tasty / was / the food / not / enough
15   London / Film / I never miss the / Festival
16   is dying / shipbuilding / industry / British / the
17   in the world / it used to be / largest / the
18   correct / is / completely / always / her homework
19   it was / we expected / more / than / difficult
20   nice person / just / really / met a / we have

19.2 The correct form (PBEG 64; 67; 68, appendix 8)

Fill in the gap with the correct form of the word in brackets.
Example: I can run _____ (fast) than you.
Answer: I can run <u>faster</u> than you.

1 I was very _____ (careful) when I opened the door.

2 I opened the door very _____ (careful).

3 I was much more _____ (careful) than I usually am.

4 We had to work very _____ (hard) in those days.

5 They were _____ (hard) times for all of us.

6 We _____ (hard) had enough to eat.

7 When the war came, we had to work even _____ (hard).

8 Diamonds are the _____ (hard) stones in the world.

9 I can explain it to you very _____ (simple).

10 He's _____ (probable) at home now.

11 We arrived _____ (early) and had to wait half an hour.

12 But we weren't the first. Some people arrived even _____ (early).

13 The _____ (early) people of all had arrived three hours before us.

14 I hope you are feeling _____ (good) than last week.

15 You'll have to do it a lot _____ (fast) than that next time.

16 Australia is much too _____ (far) away for a holiday.

17 We need to go somewhere much _____ (near).

18 I just can't go any _____ (far). You'll have to leave me here.

19 He gets the _____ (much) money because he's the _____ (good) player.

19.3 Almost / hardly / just / really (PBEG 67)

Fill in the gap with **almost, hardly, just** *or* **really**.

Example: We were too late for the train. We _____ missed it.
Answer: We were too late for the train. We just missed it.

1 This game is _____ nice. I like it very much.

2 Speak up! I can only _____ hear you.

3 This game is stupid. I _____ don't like it.

4 It's OK but it's rather boring. I don't _____ like it.

5 I passed the exam. But I was so careless that I _____ didn't.

6 That's incredible! I can _____ believe it.

7 Don't you like the food? You've _____ eaten anything.

8 Don't you like the food? You've eaten _____ nothing.

9 I _____ missed the train. It left as soon as I got on.

10 I was so happy that I _____ noticed the rain.

11 I was so happy that I didn't _____ notice the rain.

12 I was so happy, I _____ danced in the rain. I didn't care how wet I got.

19.4 *Too / enough / very* (PBEG 67)

Fill in the gap with **too, enough** *or* **very**.

Example: Thank you. That was _____ kind of you.
Answer: Thank you. That was <u>very</u> kind of you.

1 Hello! You're looking _____ well today.
2 We didn't leave early _____.
3 The weather forecast says it's going to be _____ cold today.
4 It's much _____ cold to go swimming.
5 But if we take _____ warm clothes to put on afterwards, it'll be alright.
6 No, it's not nearly warm _____.
7 Anyway, I'm not feeling _____ well.
8 It's _____ late to go out now.
9 Have we got _____ milk for the weekend?
10 Yes, in fact I think we've got _____ much; some of it will go bad.
11 I love you _____ much.
12 And I think you are _____ nice.

19.5 *Forms for comparison* (PBEG 68; appendix 7)

Fill in the gap with [word] + **-er / -est** *or* **more / most** + *[word]*.

Example: Travelling by car is _____ (convenient) than by train.
Answer: Travelling by car is <u>more convenient</u> than by train.
Example: I think it would be _____ (quick) to go by train.
Answer: I think it would be <u>quicker</u> to go by train.

1 This is a lot _____ (comfortable) than going by car.
2 It's also a lot _____ (safe).
3 And it's much _____ (fast) too.
4 That's the _____ (ridiculous) thing I've ever heard.
5 This must be the _____ (slow) way to travel that there is.
6 Anyway, your camel is _____ (big) than mine.
7 In my opinion, nothing in the world could be _____ (uncomfortable).
8 I wish I had a _____ (large) camel.
9 Why did we choose the _____ (hot) day in the year to go on this journey?
10 This is the _____ (unpleasant) trip I've ever been on.
11 It would have been much _____ (easy) to go by car.
12 The grass is always _____ (green) on the other side of the hill.

19.6 Phrases for comparison (PBEG 68–70)

Fill in the gap with **as, by, in, little, of, than** *or* **the** *or leave it blank.*

Example: The Nile is longer _____ any other river _____ the world.

Answer: The Nile is longer <u>than</u> any other river <u>in</u> the world.

1 This exercise is a _____ easier _____ the last exercise.
2 It's not quite _____ difficult.
3 I think it's _____ easiest one _____ this section.
4 It's certainly much _____ easier _____ I first thought.
5 You can do it _____ quickly _____ any _____ the others.
6 It's much _____ quicker to do _____ the others.
7 It's _____ far _____ simplest exercise.
8 I hope the next exercise is _____ easy _____ this one.

19.7 Sentences of comparison (PBEG 68–70)

Write sentences of comparison which have exactly the same meaning as the sentences above them.

Example: Edinburgh was 6°C yesterday. London was 16°C yesterday.
Answer: London was <u>much warmer than Edinburgh yesterday.</u>

England is a good team. Ireland is a very good team.

1 Ireland is _____.
2 England is _____.

Canada is not a very good team. The USA is not at all good.

3 The USA _____.

The USA is not a good team at all. Ireland is very good.

4 Ireland is _____.
5 The USA _____.

John has got £10. Maria has got £15. Peter has got £95.

6 John has _____ Maria.
7 John has _____ Peter.
8 Maria has _____ John.
9 Peter has _____ Maria.
10 Peter is _____ the other two.
11 Peter is _____ of the three.

In Athens, you need £60 a week, in London £120 and in Brussels £130.

12 Athens is _____ London or Brussels.

13 London is _____ Brussels.

14 The cost of living in Brussels _____ London.

15 Brussels _____ Athens.

16 You don't need _____ to live in Athens _____ Brussels.

19.8 The correct meaning (PBEG 64–70)

Complete each sentence so that it means the same as the sentence just above it.
Example: Athens is hotter than Rome.
Answer: Rome is not <u>as hot as Athens</u>.

1 She is an extremely good English teacher.

   She teaches _____.

2 No car on earth is faster than this one.

   This is _____.

3 I've never seen such an exciting match.

   That was _____.

4 This shelf is too small for these books.

   These books _____.

5 This shelf is too small for these books.

   This shelf is not _____.

6 The Portuguese team is a little faster than the Spanish.

   The Spanish team is not _____.

7 She hardly had time to finish.

   She almost _____.

8 This car is the cheapest you can get.

   This car costs _____.

9 In the world of sport, he gets paid the most.

   He gets paid more _____.

10 John and Maria are exactly the same. They are both intelligent.

John is _____ _____ .

11 It rains much more in Kenya than it does in Somalia.

It doesn't rain _____ .

12 She almost failed the exam.

She only _____ .

20

TALKING ABOUT TIME

This section gives you practice with the prepositions and adverbs that we use to talk about when, how much time and how often.

NOTE For practice with clock time and dates, look at Extra Exercises 10 and 11.

20.1 Word order (PBEG 72; 73)

Change the order of the words or groups of words to make a correct sentence.
Example: work / late / often / I
Answer: I often work late.

1 things / usually / forget / never / I
2 in the evening / out / often / go / we
3 day / a / factory works / 24 hours / this
4 a / take / ever / don't you / break?
5 before / crossing the road / always / carefully / look
6 the day school finished / ever / won't / I / forget
7 year / times / a market here / three / a / there is
8 in a shop / closed down / after / I worked / the factory

20.2 Ago or before (PBEG 71)

*Fill in the gap with **ago** or **before**.*
Example: It's six o'clock. The shop closed half an hour _____.
Answer: It's six o'clock. The shop closed half an hour <u>ago</u>.

1 You can't go to the film now; it started half an hour _____.
2 We got to the cinema at six but the film had started half an hour _____.
3 I have seen that man _____.
4 I saw him about a week _____.
5 Maria left ten minutes _____.
6 Maria left ten minutes _____ you came in.
7 200 years _____, people didn't have electric light.
8 People didn't have electric light 200 years _____.

20.3 Late (PBEG 71)

*Fill in the gap with **late, later** or **lately**.*
Example: I have been ill _____.
Answer: I have been ill <u>lately</u>.

1 We had breakfast and left the house ten minutes _____.
2 We were ten minutes _____ for school.
3 The teacher asked us why we were _____.
4 Actually, school has not been very pleasant _____.
5 I have been staying at home _____.
6 Will you be at home _____?
7 Yes, I want to watch the _____ night news programme.
8 I wish spring would come. It's very _____ this year.

20.4 Already / still / just / yet (PBEG 71)

*Fill in the gap with **already, still, just** or **yet**.*

Example: Do you _____ smoke cigarettes?
Answer: Do you <u>still</u> smoke cigarettes?

1 Have you seen that new film _____? It's very good.
2 No, I haven't seen it _____.
3 Maria's happy because she has _____ had some exciting news.
4 I've _____ been to America. I got back yesterday.
5 I've _____ been to America. I went there last year.
6 They have not _____ decided what to do.
7 They _____ haven't decided what to do.
8 They are _____ trying to decide.
9 They have _____ made a decision. I heard it on the news.
10 I've _____ spent twenty minutes on this problem and I _____ can't work it out.
11 Has Maria finished _____? That was quick!

20.5 In / on / at (PBEG 72)

*Fill in the gap with **in, on** or **at**.*

Example: I'll see you _____ half past four.
Answer: I'll see you <u>at</u> half past four.

1 _____ that time of the year, it was very hot.
2 _____ the summer, the grass turned brown in the garden.
3 John was born _____ June.
4 _____ Christmas, we all went to my grandmother's house.
5 _____ Christmas Day that year, it started to snow.
6 Will I be seeing you _____ the weekend?
7 You can always phone late _____ night.
8 _____ exactly midnight, the phone rang.
9 Presidential elections are always held _____ Tuesday.
10 The First World War ended _____ 1918.

11 I'll see you _____ lunchtime.

12 I won't be at home _____ Saturday morning, but I'll be there _____ the afternoon.

13 I was born _____ 23rd January, 1976, _____ half past seven _____ the evening.

20.6 *By* or *until* (PBEG 72)

Fill in the gap with **by** *or* **until**.

Example: _____ November, the weather had become very cold.
Answer: <u>By</u> November, the weather had become very cold.

I can't see you at half past four; I can't leave the office (**1**) _____ a quarter past four, so I can't possibly get there (**2**) _____ half past. I'll be there (**3**) _____ five o'clock. I can stay (**4**) _____ seven, then I have to leave.

5 It wasn't _____ 1950 that our village began to grow, but _____ 1965, it had become an important town.

6 We can't do anything _____ they fix the computer. They say they'll have fixed it _____ this afternoon.

20.7 *Since / for / in* (PBEG 72)

Fill in the gap with **since, for** *or* **in**.

Example: I worked _____ three hours without stopping.
Answer: I worked <u>for</u> three hours without stopping.

1 It's been raining _____ yesterday afternoon.

2 It's been raining _____ twenty hours now without stopping.

I haven't seen them (**3**) _____ ages. I last saw them (**4**) _____ 1987 and I haven't seen them (**5**) _____.

It's a long time (**6**) _____ I've been to England, but (**7**) _____ three days from now, I'll be there. I'm staying there (**8**) _____ three days.

9 I lived there _____ two whole years and _____ all that time I didn't make any friends.

10 He can see you _____ half an hour but he can't talk _____ more than a few minutes.

20.8 *The correct word* (PBEG 71–3)

Fill in the gap with one word from the list below.

by every for from never once often to twice usually then (use **then** twice)

Example: I go running _____ day.
Answer: I go running <u>every</u> day.

I'll be at work (**1**) _____ three hours this afternoon, (**2**) _____ two
(**3**) _____ five. (**4**) _____ I'll take the bus home. It (**5**) _____
takes about an hour, so I'll probably be back (**6**) _____ six. I'll see you
(**7**) _____.

(**8**) _____ a week, we have a lesson in the language laboratory. We go
there (**9**) _____ Thursday afternoon. I find the language laboratory
very useful so I (**10**) _____ miss it. In fact, I (**11**) _____ stay on
there by myself after the lesson has finished. We all like the language
lab., so we're going to ask our teacher if we can go there (**12**) _____ a
week.

20.9 *The correct meaning* (PBEG 71–3)

Complete each sentence so that it means the same as the sentence just above it.
Example: I always go to the English lessons.
Answer: I never <u>miss the English lessons.</u>

1 They are still trying to fix the car.

   They haven't _____.

2 I always get up early in the morning.

   I get up _____.

3 I always get up early in the morning.

   I never _____.

4 She never forgets my birthday.

   She always _____.

5 The shop opened at eight and closed at half past eleven.

   The shop was open _____.

6 He finally arrived at half past three.

   He didn't _____.

7 I only watch TV occasionally.

   I don't _____.

8 Twice a week, on Tuesdays and Thursdays, I go to evening classes.

   Every _____.

9 We last met in January last year.

   We haven't _____.

10 Before we went to the concert, we went to the café.

   We went to the concert _____.

11 Before we went to the concert, we went to the café.

   We went to the café and _____.

12 Before I came to live here, I lived in the city.

   I've lived here ever _____.

21

BASIC PREPOSITIONS OF PLACE

In order to talk about the position of something or somebody, we usually use prepositions (small words such as **in, on**, etc.). The correct preposition to use depends not only on the position (place) but also on how exact we want to be.

21.1 *Geographical position* (PBEG 74; 75.1)

*Fill in the gap with **in, on, at, to** or **off**.*
Example: Mount Everest is _____ Nepal.
Answer: Mount Everest is <u>in</u> Nepal.

1 Bolivia is a country _____ South America.
2 I live _____ the country.
3 The town of Boston is _____ the north-east of the USA.
4 Boston is _____ the east coast of North America.
5 Boston lies _____ the north-east of the city of New York.
6 My parents live _____ Godfrey Avenue.
7 They live _____ 28 Godfrey Avenue.
8 Puerto Rico is an island _____ the Caribbean Sea.
9 Puerto Rico is situated just _____ the coast of North America.
10 My father's parents live _____ the mountains.
11 London stands _____ the river Thames.
12 We stayed _____ a small Greek island for our holidays.

21.2 *At or in* (PBEG 76)

*Fill in the gap with **at** or **in**.*
Example: Maria broke her leg. She's _____ hospital.
Answer: Maria broke her leg. She's <u>in</u> hospital.

1 Maria's _____ the airport, waiting for John to arrive.
2 There are two different buildings _____ the airport: one for arrivals, and one for departures.
3 It was really hot _____ the Arrivals Building.
4 There were hundreds of people waiting _____ Gate No. 3.
5 There's a group playing _____ the Grand Café this evening.
6 There were lots of people _____ the café and I couldn't see an empty seat.

7 I was _____ university for five years.

8 Could you just wait _____ that office there, please?

21.3 *In* or *on* (PBEG 79)

Fill in the gap with **in** *or* **on**.

Example: He shook my hand and slapped me _____ the back.
Answer: He shook my hand and slapped me <u>on</u> the back.

1 What have you got _____ your hand?

2 What is that red mark _____ your hand?

3 That's him, over there _____ the blue pullover.

4 It's warm so I won't put my pullover _____.

5 The glasses are _____ that cupboard there.

6 The coffee is _____ that shelf there.

7 He's so stupid. He has nothing at all _____ his head.

8 What's that strange thing he's wearing _____ his head?

9 There's a lot of dust _____ the TV screen.

10 There was a faulty wire _____ the TV.

11 The clothes are already _____ the washing machine. You can turn it _____ now.

21.4 *At / in / on* (PBEG 75–8)

Fill in the gap with **at**, **in** *or* **on**.

Example: My house is _____ the corner.
Answer: My house is <u>on the corner</u>.

1 I live _____ a block of flats.

2 It's just _____ the end of the street.

3 Our flat is _____ the seventh floor.

4 He was sitting _____ the front of the bus.

5 He was sitting _____ front of me.

6 Spring is coming. Look at the leaves _____ the trees.

7 The birds were singing _____ the trees.

8 The cat waited _____ the foot of the tree.

9 Be careful when you drive. There's ice _____ the road.

10 There are several supermarkets _____ this street.

11 There's a restaurant _____ the top of the hotel.

12 There's a TV aerial _____ the top of the building.

13 There's a chair _____ the corner. Can you get it?

14 There was a big lorry _____ my right.

15 They were driving very fast _____ the left hand lane.

16 I was trapped _____ the middle.

22

PREPOSITIONS OF PLACE AND MOVEMENT

Some prepositions can be used to talk about both the position (place) and the movement of something or somebody. Other prepositions can be used only for position or only for movement.

22.1 In / into / to (PBEG 74–6)

Fill in the gap with **in, into** *or* **to**.

Example: I got the bus _____ school today.
Answer: I got the bus <u>to</u> school today.

1 We drove _____ Greece and back last year.
2 We went through passport control and drove _____ Greece.
3 We drove about _____ Greece for several days.
4 We decided to go _____ the river for a swim.
5 When we got there, we dived straight _____ the water.
6 I had a nice time _____ town yesterday.
7 The clothes looked nice, so I went _____ the shop to buy them.
8 I pushed open the big doors and walked _____.
9 Three men stood next to the car for several minutes. Then they got _____.
10 Then another man came along and jumped _____ the car.
11 They sat _____ the car for some time before they drove off.
12 I walked all the way _____ school this morning.

22.2 To / at / from (PBEG 74–6)

Fill in the gap with **to, at** *or* **from** *or leave it blank.*

Example: I reached _____ home very late.
Answer: I reached home <u>very</u> late. (leave it blank)

1 Maria's not here. She's gone _____ the airport.
2 She went _____ there an hour ago.
3 I went _____ the airport at four o'clock.
4 I arrived _____ the airport at four o'clock.
5 I reached _____ the airport at four o'clock.
6 It was autumn and the leaves were falling _____ the trees.
7 You can see for miles _____ the top of this building.

8 The car drove straight _____ me. He can't have seen me.

9 We left _____ the airport at six.

10 We got _____ home at half past.

11 It's only four miles _____ door _____ door.

22.3 *Some prepositions of movement* (PBEG 74; 75; 78)

Fill in the gap with **across, into, past, round, through** *or* **towards**.

Example: I looked _____ the window to see if they were there.

Answer: I looked <u>through</u> the window to see if they were there.

1 He drove right _____ us without stopping. Perhaps he didn't see us.

2 Arrest him! He drove right _____ those red lights.

3 He looked right _____ me as if I wasn't there.

4 There was a man walking _____ me. It was obvious he wanted to talk.

5 He looked deep _____ my eyes.

6 We stared at each other _____ the table.

7 It's difficult to swim _____ that river. It's a long way.

8. It takes about five minutes to walk _____ the block.

9 I had a warm jacket on but the cold wind cut straight _____ it.

10 It was very difficult to see _____ the thick fog.

11 I could see _____ their living room from the street.

12 Look both ways before you walk _____ the road.

We walked **(13)** _____ the museum doors, **(14)** _____ the guards and **(15)** _____ a big room. When John saw the dinosaur in the corner, he ran straight **(16)** _____ it.

22.4 *Off / out / out of* (PBEG 75.2; 76.2; 78.2; 79)

Fill in the gap with **off, out** *or* **out of**.

Example: I was _____ all day yesterday.

Answer: I was <u>out</u> all day yesterday.

1 Get _____ the TV. You might break it.

2 Get _____ that armchair. That's where I always sit.

3 Leave the room. Get _____ now before I hit you.

4 Let's get the photos _____ and have a look at them.

5 The label had come _____ the tin and I didn't know how to cook it.

6 I poured the soup _____ the tin.

7 The key was stuck. I couldn't get it _____ the lock.

8 You get _____ the bus at the next stop.

9 He fell _____ a ladder and hurt himself.

10 When I opened my bag, all the money fell _____ onto the floor.

11 The door was locked from the inside so I climbed _____ the window.

12 This button has come _____ my shirt.

13 Take your shoes _____ before you come in here.

14 When I came _____ the library, the sun was shining brightly.

15 They came _____ to say goodbye to us. As we drove _____, they waved.

22.5 Over / above / up / on top of
(PBEG 76.3; 77; 79.3)

*Fill in the gap with **over, above, up** or **on top of**.*

Example: I got _____ off the floor.
Answer: I got <u>up</u> off the floor.

1 You can wear a pullover _____ your shirt.

2 If you put the box _____ the wardrobe, nobody will see it.

3 Why don't we hang that picture _____ the wardrobe?

4 I reached the first floor by climbing _____ the ladder.

5 The ladder was lying on the ground. I stepped carefully _____ it and walked on.

6 This town is 2,000 metres _____ sea level.

7 When he saw us, the cat jumped _____ the table and sat there.

8 When he saw us, the cat jumped right _____ the table and landed on the sofa on the other side.

22.6 Under / below / down / underneath
(PBEG 76.3; 77; 79.3)

*Fill in the gap with **under, below, down** or **underneath**. Use each word only once.*

Example: I put my key _____ the mat.
Answer: I put my key <u>under</u> the mat.

1 We were so high up, we could see the birds flying _____ us.

2 When it started to rain, we sheltered _____ a tree.

3 Suddenly, a cat slid _____ the tree and landed at the bottom.

4 Then it tried to hide _____ a pile of old leaves.

23

HOW AND WHY

We use adverbs or prepositions to talk about how something is done. To talk about purpose, reason and consequence, we often need a word or phrase that connects two ideas.

23.1 Word order (PBEG 80–82)

Change the order of the words or groups of words to make a correct sentence or correct sentences. Put in punctuation and use capital letters when necessary.

Example: a doctor / to / you have to study / be / hard
Answer: You have to study hard to be a doctor.

Example: it is better / houses are expensive / therefore / to get a flat
Answer: Houses are expensive. Therefore it is better to get a flat.

1 straight to bed / we went / because / were tired / we
2 straight to bed / we / so / were tired / we went
3 straight to bed / we / because / were tired / we went
4 straight to bed / we were / so / tired / we went / that
5 plastic / is / of / this chair / made
6 a traffic jam and / there was / I was late / as / a result
7 quietly / nobody / so that / he spoke / would hear him
8 quietly / so / it was playing / nobody could hear it / that
9 there was enough room / I moved the bookshelf / so that / for the TV
10 there would be lots of people there / early / because / we left
11 most people / there is no public transport / as a result / have cars
12 early / I took a taxi / I'd arrive / so that
13 early / we got good seats / we left / because
14 early / we got good seats / we left / so
15 I took an umbrella / I expected it / as / to rain
16 I took an umbrella / I expected it / so / to rain

23.2 By / for / to / with (PBEG 80; 81)

Fill in the gap with by, for, to or with.

Example: These houses are made _____ cement.
Answer: These houses are made <u>with</u> cement.

1 You open the back of the radio _____ a screwdriver.
2 You open the back of the radio _____ using a screwdriver.
3 You can get there _____ bus but it takes a long time.
4 This pipe here is _____ gas.

5 These are special envelopes _____ sending documents safely.

6 We kept the document safe _____ sending it in a special envelope.

7 _____ a car, you can stop whenever you want.

8 _____ car, the journey doesn't take long.

9 We use this key _____ open the office door.

10 This key here is _____ opening the office door.

11 You can open the office door _____ this key here.

12 The office door can be opened _____ using this key here.

13 Medical students get experience _____ working in hospitals.

14 Medical students work in hospitals _____ get experience.

15 What did you do that _____? Now, we'll never find it.

16 What did you cut that _____? You can't have used scissors.

23.3 Because / so / as a result (PBEG 81; 82)

*Fill in the gap with **because, so** or **as a result**.*

Example: The orange trees had been damaged. _____ oranges were expensive.

Answer: The orange trees had been damaged. <u>As a result</u>, oranges were expensive.

1 We had to take a taxi _____ we missed the bus.

2 We had to take a taxi _____ we could arrive in time.

3 We left early _____ we didn't have to hurry.

4 We walked slowly _____ we didn't have to hurry.

5 We left early. _____ we didn't have to hurry.

6 I have a bad back _____ I don't play tennis any more.

7 I don't play tennis any more _____ I have a bad back.

8 I often go to that café _____ I like the atmosphere there.

9 That café has the nicest atmosphere _____ I usually go there.

10 The plane was two hours late _____ the fog was very thick.

11 The plane was delayed for two hours _____ we had a cup of coffee.

12 His passport was not in order. _____ he was not allowed to enter the country.

23.4 So or such (PBEG 82.4)

*Fill in the gap with **so** or **such**.*

Example: I was _____ tired that I fell asleep immediately.
Answer: I was <u>so</u> tired that I fell asleep immediately.

1 I had _____ a lot to do at home that I was late for work.

2 I had _____ much to do at home that I was late for work.

3   Where did you learn _____ good English?
4   Japanese is _____ a difficult language to learn.
5   Japanese is _____ difficult that few people learn it well.
6   The question was _____ hard I couldn't answer it.
7   It was _____ a hard question I couldn't answer it.
8   There were _____ many students they couldn't all find a seat.

23.5   So / so that / so . . . that (PBEG 81; 82)

Use **so,** **so that** *or* **so . . . that** *in the correct place(s) to make a sentence. Put in punctuation and use capital letters when necessary.*

Example: he had much money he didn't know what to do with it
Answer: He had <u>so</u> much money <u>that</u> he didn't know what to do with
         it.

1   they were very tall it was easy to find them
2   he is tall he has to wear special clothes
3   they were wearing strange clothes it was easy to find them
4   they put on strange clothes it would be easy to find them
5   she did well in her exam she won first prize
6   the lecture was boring I fell asleep
7   I made a list I wouldn't forget anything
8   I had forgotten something I had to go home and get it

23.6   Connecting ideas (PBEG 80–82)

Fill in the gap with one word from the list below.

as a result   because   by   for   so   so that   such   that   to

I couldn't get in (**1**) _____ the front door (**2**) _____ it was locked
(**3**) _____ I walked around the house (**4**) _____ see if any windows
were open. An upstairs window was open (**5**) _____ I got the ladder. I
thought I could get in (**6**) _____ climbing through the window.
(**7**) _____ everybody was asleep, I was very quiet (**8**) _____ nobody
would wake up. I was nearly at the top when the ladder fell sideways.
(**9**) _____ I lost my balance and fell into the garden. This made
(**10**) _____ a terrible noise (**11**) _____ everybody in the house woke
up. My brother opened the door and asked me if I knew what a front
doorbell was (**12**) _____.

23.7   The correct meaning (PBEG 80–82)

Complete each sentence so that it means the same as the sentence just above it.
Example: He didn't go out because he was ill.
Answer: He was ill <u>so he didn't go out.</u>

1 We couldn't take the plane because it was too expensive.

The plane was too expensive _____.

2 Cigarettes are very expensive now so I can't afford them.

I can't afford _____.

3 Cigarettes are very expensive now so I can't afford them.

Because _____.

4 Cigarettes are very expensive now so I can't afford them.

Cigarettes are so _____.

5 I put it next to the door so that I wouldn't forget it.

So that _____.

6 I put it next to the door so that I wouldn't forget it.

Because _____.

7 It was such a difficult exam that nobody passed it.

The _____.

8 I couldn't hear what he said because the wind was blowing so strongly.

The wind was _____.

9 I couldn't hear what he said because the wind was so strong.

It was _____.

10 We left early in order to get good seats.

We left early so _____.

11 The way for us to make sure it arrives is to send it express.

We can make sure it arrives _____.

12 You have to break eggs to make an omelette.

You can't _____.

24

SIMILAR AND OPPOSITE IDEAS

The correct way to connect two or more ideas depends on what kind of connection they have – are they the same as each other or are they opposite to each other? It can also depend on the length of the statements.

24.1 And or or (PBEG 83)

*Fill in the gap with **and** or **or**.*

Example: I don't like chicken _____ beef.
Answer: I don't like chicken or beef.

1 I went shopping in the morning _____ the afternoon yesterday.
2 But I didn't do any housework in the morning _____ the afternoon.
3 He's taken John _____ Maria for a walk. They're in the park.
4 He didn't take John _____ Maria for a walk yesterday. They stayed at home.
5 He didn't take John for a walk _____ Maria for a walk yesterday.
6 John _____ Maria didn't go for a walk yesterday. They stayed at home.
7 She's got a bicycle _____ a car. She's lucky.
8 He hasn't got a bicycle _____ a car. He walks everywhere.

24.2 And / also / both / so / too / as well
(PBEG 58.2; 83)

*Fill in the gap with **and, also, both, so** or **too / as well**.*

Example: He has a car. He _____ has a bicycle.
Answer: He has a car. He also has a bicycle.

1 I've got three brothers here _____ another brother in America.
2 I _____ have a brother who lives in America.
3 I enjoy science fiction books. My wife likes them _____.
4 I enjoy science fiction books _____ _____ does my wife.
5 My wife _____ I _____ enjoy science fiction books.
6 I have a regular job but I _____ work in the evenings.
7 We've had trouble with the fridge _____ the cooker _____ our heater have stopped working _____.
8 The heater's broken down _____ _____ has the fridge.
9 _____ the heater _____ the fridge have broken down.
10 The fridge, the heater _____ the cooker have all broken down.

24.3 *Either / or / neither / nor* (PBEG 58.2; 83)

*Fill in the gap with **either, or, neither** or **nor**.*

Example: You must do _____ question one _____ question two.
Answer: You must do either question one or question two.

1 The heater isn't working. The fridge isn't working _____.
2 I can't get the heater _____ the fridge to work.
3 I can't get _____ the heater _____ the fridge to work.
4 _____ the heater _____ the fridge is working.
5 The fridge isn't working and _____ is the heater.
6 I don't understand it _____.

24.4 *Although / but / however / on the other hand* (PBEG 84)

*Fill in the gap with **although, but, however** or **on the other hand**.*

Example: Country life is peaceful. _____ it can be boring.
Answer: Country life is peaceful. However, it can be boring.

1 His work is slow _____ sure.
2 _____ he works slowly, he never makes a mistake.
3 He works slowly _____ he never makes a mistake.
4 He works rather slowly. _____, he never makes a mistake.
5 _____ smoking might protect your teeth, it is still bad for you.
6 Smoking might protect your teeth. _____, it is still bad for you.
7 You could phone the dentist and make an appointment. _____, you could go there and wait.
8 You could phone the dentist and make an appointment. _____, it would be quicker if you went there.

24.5 *And / both / but / either / or* (PBEG 58.2; 83; 84)

*Fill in the gap with **and, or, but, either** or **both**.*

Example: We learn _____ English _____ Spanish _____ not _____.

Answer: We learn either English or Spanish but not both.

1 We could _____ spend the money _____ we could save it.
2 We could spend the money _____ it would be better to save it.
3 I could save the money _____ I really want to spend it.
4 The red dress _____ the blue dress are _____ nice.
5 I like the red dress more _____ the blue one is cheaper.
6 The blue one is cheaper _____ it doesn't look so nice.
7 The blue one is cheaper _____ it is probably easier to wash.
8 Which one shall I buy? The red one _____ the blue one?

24.6 *The correct meaning* (PBEG 83; 84)

Complete each sentence so that it means the same as the sentence(s) just above it.
Example: Maria and John like fruit.
Answer: Maria likes fruit. John <u>also likes fruit</u>. (. . . <u>does too</u> / . . . <u>does as well</u>.)

1 John should be home by now. Maria should be home by now.

Both _____.

2 John should be home by now. Maria should be home by now.

John should be home by now and so _____.

3 He is slow and careless.

He is neither _____.

4 I think it would be better to watch the match on TV.

I would _____.

5 Although the weather is fine, it is very cold.

The weather _____.

6 We cannot see both the film and the football match.

We can see _____.

7 Maria and John have lost their bags.

Maria has lost _____.

8 Maria and John have lost their bags.

Maria can't find _____.

25

SEQUENCE AND CONDITIONS

We often need to use connecting words to show which of two events happened first. We use the word **if** to introduce a condition. Some conditions are real (what we say in the condition is possibly true) and some conditions are unreal (what we say in the condition is not true). The correct verb formation is very important when talking about sequence and conditions.

25.1 *Understanding sequence* (PBEG 85)

Read the sentences below. Each describes two events: John arriving and having lunch. Which event happened first? Or did they both happen at the same time?

1 After we had lunch, John arrived.
2 John arrived after we had lunch.
3 John arrived. After that, we had lunch.
4 Before John arrived, we had lunch.
5 John arrived when we were having lunch.
6 While we were having lunch, John arrived.
7 We had had lunch when John arrived.
8 We had lunch when John arrived.

25.2 **When / while / and** (PBEG 85)

Fill in the gap with **when, while** *or* **and.**
Example: I sat down _____ drank my coffee.
Answer: I sat down <u>and</u> drank my coffee.

1 I washed up _____ put the dishes away.
2 _____ I washed up, Maria put the dishes away.
3 _____ I had washed up, Maria put the dishes away.
4 I washed up _____ Maria was putting the dishes away.
5 I washed up _____ then Maria put the dishes away.
6 I put the dishes away _____ I finished washing up.
7 I was doing the washing up _____ Maria broke a plate.
8 _____ I was doing the washing up, Maria broke a plate.

25.3 **After** or **after that** (PBEG 85)

Fill in the gap with **after** *or* **after that**.

Example: I had my dinner. _____ I wrote some letters.
Answer: I had my dinner. <u>After that</u> I wrote some letters.

1 _____ I washed up, I put the dishes away.
2 I put the dishes away _____ I had washed up.
3 I did the washing up. _____ I put the dishes away.
4 You do the washing up first. I'll put the dishes away _____.

25.4 *Showing sequence clearly* (PBEG 85)

Complete each sentence using the words just above it.

Example: having bath / phone rang
Answer: I was <u>having a bath when the phone rang</u>.

1 watching TV / doorbell rang

  I was _____.

2 watching TV / doorbell rang

  While _____.

3 watching TV / doorbell rang

  The _____.

4 doorbell rang / turned off TV

  I turned _____.

5 doorbell rang / turned off TV

  When _____.

6 turned off TV / opened door

  Before _____.

7 turned off TV / opened door

  I turned _____.

8 turned off TV / opened door

  I opened _____.

25.5 *Understanding conditions* (PBEG 86)

Read each sentence and answer the questions below. Answer 'Yes', 'No' or 'Possibly'.

If I get the money, I'll buy a car.
1   Will I buy a car?
2   Will I get the money?

If I had enough money, I would have a car.
3   Do I have a car?
4   Do I have enough money?

If I had got that money, I would've bought a car.
5   Did I get the money?
6   Did I buy a car?

If I hadn't got that money, I wouldn't have been able to buy a car.
7   Did I get the money?
8   Did I buy a car?

25.6 *The correct verb formation* (PBEG 86)

Fill in the gap with the correct formation of the verb in brackets.

Example: If she _____ (talk) on the phone, she probably didn't hear the doorbell.

Answer: If she <u>was talking</u> on the phone, she probably didn't hear the doorbell.

1   If it _____ (rain) tomorrow, we can't go out.
2   If it _____ (not rain), we could go out now. What a pity!
3   Unless it _____ (stop) raining soon, we can't go out at all.
4   If it _____ (not rain) yesterday, we could have gone out.
5   If it _____ (not rain) yesterday, they probably went out.
6   If he _____ (not leave) already, he'll be in his office.
7   If he _____ (not leave) already, he'd be in his office.
8   Do you mind if I _____ (open) the window?
9   Would you mind if I _____ (open) the window?
10 If they _____ (have) a car, they can get there easily.
11 If only they _____ (have) a car, they could get there easily.
12 If they _____ (have) a car with them yesterday, they must have got there very quickly.

25.7 *Making conditional sentences* (PBEG 86)

Write a sentence with a condition in it for each situation described below.
Begin with 'If I'. More than one answer is possible.

Example: I passed the exam; that's how I got this boring job.
Answer: If I hadn't passed the exam, I might have got a more
         interesting job.
         If I'd failed the exam, I wouldn't have got this boring job.

1 I can't go on holiday because I spent all my money on clothes.
2 I can't go on holiday because I spend all my money on cigarettes.
3 I passed the exam and here I am at university.
4 I hope to see Maria there so that I can tell her the news.

25.8 *The correct meaning* (PBEG 85–6)

Complete each sentence so that it means the same as the sentence just above it.
Example: I can't meet you because I don't have the time.
Answer: If <u>I had more time, I could meet you.</u>

1 Get out or I'll punch you on the nose.

   If you _____.

2 If John has got his key with him, we can get in.

   Unless _____.

3 First turn the power off and then correct the fault.

   Turn _____.

4 I'll have another cup of coffee; then I'll leave.

   Before _____.

5 I'll have another cup of coffee; then I'll leave.

   I'll leave after _____.

6 John might be coming to the party, so we can arrange it then.

   If _____.

7 John didn't come to the party, so we couldn't arrange it then.

   If _____.

8 If you have a terrible toothache, why don't you see the dentist?

   If I _____.

9 I'd like to bring my baby with me; is that alright?

Would you _____.

10 I'd like to bring my baby with me; is that alright?

Is it alright _____.

11 I would introduce you to him but I can't remember his name.

If _____.

12 I didn't see you there; that's why I didn't say hello.

I would have _____.

EXTRA EXERCISES

Here are some more exercises on different areas of grammar, especially ones that often cause problems.

1 Apostrophe s ('s) (PBEG 17; 49)

What does 's stand for in these sentences: is, has or the genitive?

Example: John's bicycle's been stolen.
Answer: John's (genitive) bicycle has been stolen.
Example: What's your name?
Answer: What is your name?

1 John's a student.
2 John's been a student for two years.
3 John's teacher told him to work harder.
4 John's wasting his time.
5 John's been wasting his time ever since he got there.
6 John's tired.
7 John's tired legs couldn't take him any further.
8 The shop's closed on Sundays.
9 The shop's closed its meat counter.
10 John's father's going to see what's happened.

2 Apostrophe d ('d) (PBEG 17; 36.4)

What does 'd stand for in these sentences: had or would?

Example: I'd like to, if only I'd enough time.
Answer: I would like to, if only I had enough time.

1 I'd like to go.
2 I'd go if I could.
3 He'd gone the year before.
4 What'd you do in my position?
5 He'd have gone if he'd had the opportunity.
6 I'd better work but I'd rather go swimming instead.

3 More tag questions (PBEG 12; 27.2; 34.1; 36; 37.1; 38.1)

Complete the sentence with a tag question.

Example: You won't lose it, _____?
Answer: You won't lose it, will you?

1 You must try harder, _____?
2 You will be careful, _____?
3 They can't have got lost, _____?

4 We'll have to take a taxi, _____?

5 You wouldn't do that, _____?

6 You'd help me, _____?

7 She shouldn't have done that, _____?

8 You couldn't lend me some money, _____?

9 You don't have to go already, _____?

10 He's going to England, _____?

11 We've got to go now, _____?

12 We'd better be going now, _____?

13 They had to go by train, _____?

14 They weren't able to get a taxi, _____?

15 He didn't use to play for us, _____?

16 He used to play for another team, _____?

4 *Used to* / *past simple* / *past continuous*
(PBEG 21.2; 23.2; 38.1; 40.1)

Fill in the gap with **used to**, *the past simple or the past continuous formation, using the verb in brackets.*

Example: When I was a boy, I _____ (play) football every day.
Answer: When I was a boy, I <u>used to</u> play football every day.

1 This new teacher is awful. I _____ not _____ (understand) anything he said today.

2 Our teacher last year was awful too. I _____ not _____ (understand) anything he said either.

3 The teacher before that was very good. I always _____ (understand) everything she said.

4 When I went to London in 1980, I _____ (stay) at the Regency Hotel for a week.

5 I _____ (stay) at the Regency Hotel every time I went to London.

6 I _____ (stay) at the Regency Hotel when I heard the news.

7 I _____ (not be) keen on cars but now I'm a fanatic.

8 Twenty years ago, people _____ (talk) to each other. But now they just watch TV.

5 *Verb formations for future time* (PBEG 41)

Fill in the gap with **will, be going to**, *the present simple or the present continuous formation, using the verb in brackets. Sometimes, more than one answer is possible.*

Example: I'm going to England. My plane _____ (leave) this evening.
Answer: I'm going to England. My plane <u>leaves</u> this evening. (or <u>is</u> <u>leaving</u>)

1 I'm tired. I think I _____ (have) a rest.
2 Don't come round after lunch. I _____ (have) a rest.
3 Don't come round after lunch. She _____ (have) a music lesson.
4 _____ you _____ (do) anything this evening?

The President (5) _____ (come) to our town today and everybody
(6) _____ (hope) to get a good look at him. It looks like the weather
(7) _____ (be) good.

I (8) _____ (see) him tomorrow. He (9) _____ (come) to the office.
So I (10) _____ (talk) to him about the trip then if you like. Then we
(11) _____ (know) when we (12) _____ (go).

6 Active or passive with the verb *be* (PBEG 17.2; 42; 43)

Fill in the gap with the -ing form or the past participle form of the verb in brackets.
Example: My car has been _____ (steal).
Answer: My car has been <u>stolen</u>.

1 I was _____ (try) to listen to the news.
2 I was very _____ (surprise) to hear the news.
3 The news was very _____ (surprise).
4 Maria was _____ (help) John.
5 Maria was _____ (help) by John.
6 They have been _____ (repair) the car.
7 The car has been _____ (repair).
8 Thirty people have been _____ (invite) to the party.
9 They are _____ (invite) thirty people to the party.
10 Thirty people are _____ (invite) to the party.
11 The children are _____ (grow) quickly, aren't they?
12 The tea plant is _____ (grow) in India.

7 Singular or plural (PBEG 4; 47; 48; 55–8)

Fill in the gap with the correct form of the verb in brackets.
Example: Most bread _____ (be) made from wheat.
Answer: Most bread <u>is</u> made from wheat. (singular)

1 The best tobacco in the world _____ (come) from this region.
2 The best cigarettes in the world _____ (be) made here.
3 One of the best cigarettes in the world _____ (be) made here.
4 Some of the best cigarettes in the world _____ (be) made here.
5 Some of the best tobacco in the world _____ (come) from here.
6 Some very good cigarettes _____ (be) made here.

7 Smoking _____ (be) a cause of heart disease.

8 Smoking cigarettes _____ (be) worse than eating too much.

9 Tell me, what _____ (be) the news?

10 I don't like the job but the money _____ (be) good.

11 Our money _____ (have) come through at last.

12 Because of the weather, the police _____ (have) told drivers to be very careful.

13 All this _____ (have) made me thirsty.

14 John and Maria have done well. Both _____ (have) passed the exam.

15 No child _____ (like) going to the dentist.

16 Every one of us _____ (hate) going to the dentist.

17 All of us _____ (hate) going to the dentist.

18 Some students failed but most _____ (have) passed the exam.

19 Those _____ (be) the best!

20 Everybody _____ (know) him.

8 There / their / they're (PBEG 16; 50; 61)

Fill in the gap with **there, their** *or* **they're**.

Example: _____ is somebody in _____ house.
Answer: There is somebody in their house.

1 _____ working.

2 _____ working hours are very long.

3 _____ are working women and women who stay at home.

4 _____ very tired.

5 _____ tired legs could carry them no further.

6 I know a place where _____ are lots of good videos.

7 I know the place where _____ showing the film.

8 This is the place where they can have _____ supper.

9 _____'s John over _____.

10 _____ having a lot of trouble with _____ car.

9 Where / were / we're (PBEG 6.2; 8; 13; 16.3)

Fill in the gap with **where, were** *or* **we're**.

Example: _____ going _____ the sun shines brightly.
Answer: We're going where the sun shines brightly.

1 _____ are the books?

2 They _____ here a minute ago.

3 _____ in trouble if we can't find them.

4 _____ _____ they last night?

5 I know _____ they _____.
6 Do you know _____ we are?
7 I think _____ lost.
8 I don't even know _____ _____ going.
9 There _____ hundreds of us.

10 Telling the time (PBEG appendix 12)

How do we say this time in ordinary spoken English?
Example: 8.20 p.m.
Answer: twenty past eight in the evening

1	8.20 a.m.	7	11.00 a.m.
2	09.20	8	11.02 a.m.
3	14.20	9	02.15
4	11.15 a.m.	10	06.50
5	16.30	11	21.55
6	10.45 a.m.	12	7.35 p.m.

11 Dates (PBEG appendix 13)

How do we say these dates in ordinary English?
Example: 3rd March 1933
Answer: the third of March, nineteen thirty-three
Example: March 3 1933
Answer: March the third, nineteen thirty-three

1	1st January 1989	7	January 18th 1952
2	2 November 1987	8	October 21st 1988
3	5 June 1992	9	11th November 1918
4	25th December 1066	10	August 31st 1988
5	May 1st 1977	11	7th September 1924
6	8 April 1990	12	9 July 1951

ANSWERS

A slash (/) means an alternative answer follows. For example, '**3** will / would' means that both 'will' and 'would' are possible answers to question **3**.

A dash (–) means another part of the answer follows. For example, '**3** will – would' means that 'will' is the answer to the first part of question **3** and 'would' is the answer to the second part.

Brackets (()) means this part of the answer is possible but not necessary. For example, '**3** I (will) go there' means that both 'I go there' and 'I will go there' are possible answers to question **3**.

In many cases, a short form is possible in the answer but this has not been shown. For example, the answer to 1.3. Question 6 could be ''s been playing'.

1 THE BASIC SENTENCE

1.1 The sentence

1 No. (no verb)	6 No. (no verb)	11 Yes.	16 Yes.
2 Yes.	7 No. (no subject)	12 Yes.	17 No. (no subject
3 No. (no verb)	8 Yes.	13 No. (no verb)	18 No. (no verb)
4 Yes.	9 No. (no verb)	14 No. (no verb)	19 Yes.
5 Yes.	10 Yes.	15 Yes.	20 Yes.

1.2 The subject

1 Maria	5 Some people	9 It
2 The factory	6 you and John	10 My luggage
3 My friends	7 Rivers	11 Computers
4 they	8 The Nile	12 Oranges and apples

1.3 The verb

1 Are	5 is playing	9 like	13 was born
2 am	6 has been playing	10 helps	14 has been stolen
3 is	7 was	11 would like	15 think
4 plays	8 are	12 have seen	16 should have arrived

1.4 Singular or plural?

1 student – singular	8 Problems – plural	13 result – singular
2 students – plural	9 Travelling – singular	14 programme – singular
3 One – singular	10 Travelling – singular	15 doors – plural
4 and – plural	11 result – singular	16 doors – plural
5 Some – plural	12 results – plural	17 Director – singular
6 Money – singular		18 employees – plural
7 problems – plural		

1.5 Subject and verb agreement

1	has	6	has	11	changes	16	leave
2	think	7	does	12	will	17	sell
3	has	8	go	13	forgets	18	does
4	do	9	do	14	rains	19	is
5	find	10	have	15	have	20	is

1.6 Agreement with the verb *be* – present tense

1	is	5	are	9	is	13	am
2	am	6	is	10	am	14	are
3	am	7	is	11	Is	15	is
4	is	8	are	12	Are	16	is

1.7 Agreement with the verb *be* – past tense

1	was	4	were	7	were – was	10	were
2	was	5	was	8	was	11	were
3	were	6	were	9	were	12	was

2 MORE ABOUT THE BASIC SENTENCE

2.1 Word order

1   I went to see the doctor last week. / Last week, I went to see the doctor.
2   I was not feeling well.
3   I had a terrible headache.
4   I never usually get headaches.
5   The doctor asked me about the headache.
6   He asked a number of questions.
7   When did this headache start?
8   Does the headache keep you awake at night?
9   How long have you been feeling like this?
10   He told me what to do.
11   Take this medicine three times a day.
12   Do not work too hard.
13   I went to the chemist to get the medicine.
14   I took the medicine for four days.
15   I felt better after that.
16   I have not been to the doctor since that time. / Since that time, I have not been to the doctor.

2.2 Sentences with *not*

1   He does not play tennis.
2   I have not got a lot of money.
3   It has not been raining.
4   I am not doing many courses this term.

5 Fish do not eat fruit.
6 I did not arrive on time.
7 They were not watching TV.
8 I have not been working hard.

2.3 More sentences with **not**

1 . . . does not play football.
2 . . . do not sell drinks.
3 . . . did not pass (the) physics (exam).
4 . . . does not know John.
5 . . . did not go to France.
6 . . . have not finished the living room.
7 . . . has not been snowing.
8 . . . the plates were not (broken).

2.4 Short forms – reading

1	not	3	will not	5	have	7	is
2	is	4	will	6	has	8	has

2.5 Short forms – writing

1 I don't know if John's arrived yet.
2 I won't be able to attend tomorrow.
3 I'll see you when you've finished.
4 She's going to the party but she isn't / she's not staying late.

2.6 Types of sentences

1	statement	5	statement
2	question	6	imperative
3	question	7	statement
4	statement	8	imperative

2.7 Subject and verb

	Subject	Verb		Subject	Verb
1	Football	is	9	the robbers	arrived
2	you	Do . . . like	10	They	waited
3	It	is	11	they	went
4	you	don't . . . try	12	The bank clerks	didn't stop
5	We	are going to have	13	They	were
6	We	have	14	They	gave
7	You	can come	15	one of the robbers	was waiting
8	The bank	opened	16	the other robbers	came (out)

3 QUESTION WORDS

3.1 Word order

1 Where are you going?
2 What were they doing last night?
3 How often does he play tennis?
4 How tall are you?
5 Which university did he go to?
6 How much does that painting cost?
7 What is the weather like?
8 What kind of car is it?

3.2 Recognising question words

1 The post office workers
2 (for) two months
3 two
4 in post offices everywhere
5 Millions of letters
6 Millions
7 (for) extra work
8 The workers
9 the part-time system
10 the part-time
11 They
12 because they want the extra work themselves
13 the extra work
14 to earn more money
15 They
16 £110
17 110
18 every week
19 A postman's
20 a very low
21 very
22 The managers and workers
23 very angry
24 yesterday

3.3 Using question words

1 How old . . .?
2 When . . .?
3 How many . . .?
4 Where . . .?
5 What kind of . . .?
6 How . . .?
7 How well . . .?
8 Where . . .?
9 Why . . .?
10 How much . . .?
11 What . . .?
12 Where . . .?
13 How far . . .?
14 How . . .?
15 How long . . .?
16 Which . . .?
17 What kind of . . .?
18 Why . . .?
19 When . . .?
20 How often . . .?
21 How many . . .?
22 When . . .?

4 MAKING QUESTIONS

4.1 Word order

1 How do you do?
2 Where are you going?
3 Do you like tomatoes?

4 Why do you like tomatoes?
5 When will the match finish?
6 Where do they come from?
7 Why didn't you tell me?
8 Who does that car belong to?
9 Is there a telephone near here?
10 Do you know when we arrive?
11 What have you been doing?
12 Could you tell me the way to the bank?
13 Do you know where he is?
14 Do we have to come on Saturday?
15 I know where he lives.
16 I wonder why he hasn't come.

4.2 Making questions

1	did you	9	are you
2	Will you	10	does he come
3	won	11	will you finish
4	Can I / Could I / May I	12	do you need
5	Have you	13	broke
6	did you get	14	didn't you
7	did he tell	15	you know
8	told her	16	you tell – leaves

4.3 More questions to make

1 What is your name?
2 Where do you live?
3 What is your address?
4 When were you born?
5 Which country do you come from? / . . . have you come from?
6 Why have you come here?
7 Where do you study? / . . . are you studying?
8 How long are you staying? / . . . will you stay?

4.4 Polite questions

1 Could you tell me what your name is?
2 Could you tell me where you live?
3 Could you tell me what your address is?
4 Could you tell me when you were born?
5 Could you tell me which country you come from? / . . . you have come from?
6 Could you tell me why you have come here?
7 Could you tell me where you study? / . . . you are studying?
8 Could you tell me how long you are staying? / . . . you will stay?

4.5 What can you ask?

1 Have you found a car yet? / . . . bought a car yet?
2 Can I borrow some money from you? / Can you lend me some money?

3 Do you speak English?
4 How are you feeling?
5 Did you have a good time?
6 How much does the bus to the airport cost?
7 Do you know when the bus arrives?
8 When do the banks open?
9 Could you tell me where the bank is? / Could you tell me how to get to the bank?
10 Would you like tea or coffee? / Do you want tea or coffee?
11 Can we meet on Friday? / Can you come on Friday?
12 Who wants to come with me? / Who's coming with me?
13 Do you know if the no. 89 stops here?
14 What do you think?
15 When will it be ready?
16 Do you know which floor the accommodation office is on?

4.6 Short answers

1 Yes, I am. / No, I'm not.
2 Yes, I have. / No, I haven't.
3 Yes, it is. / No, it isn't.
4 Yes, it was. / No, it wasn't.
5 Yes, I did. / No, I didn't.
6 (My teacher) did.
7 (Maria) is.
8 Yes, I do. / No, I don't.
9 Yes, I have. / No, I haven't.
10 Yes, I can. / No, I can't.
11 (Geography) is.
12 Yes, I will. / No, I won't.

4.7 Tag questions

1 wasn't it?
2 were they?
3 isn't he?
4 aren't they?
5 can't they?
6 isn't she?
7 shouldn't he?
8 could she?
9 does he?
10 don't they?
11 will they?
12 didn't you?
13 don't you?
14 haven't you?
15 did she?
16 don't they?

5 VERB FORMS

5.1 The -s form

1 works
2 teaches
3 studies
4 goes
5 looks
6 washes
7 drives
8 worries

5.2 The -ing form

1 coming
2 arriving
3 going
4 leaving
5 travelling
6 worrying
7 walking
8 running
9 stopping
10 hoping
11 dying
12 having
13 attending
14 raining
15 getting
16 lying

17 fixing	19 winning	21 putting
18 offering	20 looking – seeing	22 living – rising

5.3 The past tense form

1	did	10	offered	19	took	28	was
2	made	11	loved	20	kept	29	told
3	baked	12	thought – tasted	21	fitted	30	had
4	left	13	felt	22	let	31	happened
5	filled	14	bought	23	went	32	spoke
6	gave	15	cost	24	saw	33	understood
7	put	16	had	25	was	34	was
8	carried	17	hit	26	took		
9	cut	18	fell – broke	27	lasted		

5.4 The past participle form

1	lent	8	got	15	taken	22	been
2	sent	9	met	16	gone	23	had
3	lost	10	taught	17	been	24	grown
4	played	11	reached	18	done	25	been
5	sold	12	left	19	broken	26	made
6	bought	13	lived	20	seen	27	told – helped
7	caught	14	known	21	given		

6 VERB FORMS IN VERB FORMATIONS

6.1 Word order

1 The weather today is terrible.
2 It has been raining for ten hours.
3 The wind is getting stronger and stronger.
4 Some trees have been blown down.
5 Lots of drivers have had accidents.
6 All ferryboats have been cancelled.
7 The last ferry journey took five hours.
8 It was waiting for two hours outside the harbour.
9 The sea was too rough to go inside.
10 The passengers were feeling very sick.
11 The boat was rocking from side to side.
12 I was travelling on that boat.
13 I did not enjoy myself.
14 I had not been feeling well.
15 I felt much worse after the journey.
16 I should have gone by plane.
17 That would have been much better.
18 I shall never travel on a ferryboat again.
19 Let me give you some advice.
20 Do not go by ferryboat in bad weather.

6.2 The verb **be**

1 been	**3** being	**5** be	**7** be – be
2 be	**4** been	**6** Being

6.3 The correct auxiliary – present

1 are	**4** have	**7** does – have	**10** has
2 Do	**5** are	**8** Has	**11** is
3 are	**6** Have	**9** is

6.4 The correct auxiliary – past

1 did	**4** did	**7** was – had	**10** Did
2 did	**5** had	**8** had	**11** had
3 was	**6** was	**9** were

6.5 The correct verb form

1 lived	**6** living	**11** eat	**16** had
2 seen	**7** been	**12** know	**17** trying
3 appear	**8** have	**13** trying	**18** find
4 died	**9** been	**14** find	**19** die
5 discovered	**10** run	**15** studying	**20** arrive

7 CONSTRUCTING VERB FORMATIONS

7.1 Present simple

1 does he know	**5** It has
2 Do you live	**6** She eats
3 She doesn't like	**7** she drives
4 It rains	**8** does she visit

7.2 Past simple

1 We arranged	**5** it didn't come	**9** crossed
2 I didn't meet	**6** I didn't know	he thought
3 happened	**7** did you get	He didn't know
4 She fell	**8** I expected – didn't you come

7.3 Present continuous

1 am writing	**5** is going
2 am using	**6** is looking
3 are . . . getting on	**7** are you coming
4 Are you working	**8** are . . . doing

7.4 Past continuous

1 he was hoping
2 were feeling
3 were you going
4 were they doing

7.5 Present perfect simple

1 They have helped
2 Have you ever been
3 He has gone
4 haven't you done
5 has he had
6 you haven't seen
7 I haven't eaten
8 have you been

7.6 Past perfect simple

1 had finished
2 had they known
3 had not expected
4 I had seen

7.7 Present perfect continuous

1 I have been coming
2 She has been playing
3 have you been doing
4 have you been waiting
5 he has been thinking
6 they have been talking
7 have been having
8 haven't they been trying

7.8 Past perfect continuous

1 They had been stealing
2 I had not been living
3 I had been doing
4 had not been feeling

8 PAST OR PRESENT

8.1 The verb do

1 Do
2 Did
3 did
4 Does
5 did
6 do
7 Do – does
8 did
9 did
10 did
11 did

8.2 The verb be

1 is
2 is
3 am
4 is
5 were
6 were
7 were/was
8 were
9 was
10 Are
11 am
12 was

8.3 The verb have

1 have
2 have
3 has
4 had
5 has
6 has
7 had
8 had

8.4 Verbs in general

1	do	9	had	17	answered	25	belonged
2	Did	10	is	18	do	26	had
3	knew	11	filled	19	run	27	was
4	has	12	do	20	am	28	have
5	speaks	13	happened	21	hate	29	finish
6	went	14	was	22	did	30	looks
7 ·	walk	15	rang	23	knew	31	wonder
8	broke	16	put	24	was	32	has

8.5 Past simple or present perfect

1	Have . . . seen	6	have . . . been	11	did . . . arrive
2	have seen	7	did . . . go	12	have done
3	did . . . sleep	8	have had	13	Did . . . enjoy
4	went	9	had	14	has promised
5	have been	10	has got	15	promised – has . . . arrived

9 SIMPLE, CONTINUOUS AND PERFECT

9.1 Present simple or present continuous

1	do . . . do	8	do . . . work	15	is boiling
2	do . . . do	9	is stealing	16	knows
3	are . . . doing	10	prefer	17	are . . . going
4	are . . . doing	11	is cooking	18	want
5	are . . . doing	12	are running	19	tastes
6	do . . . smoke	13	lies	20	am staying
7	am smoking	14	speak		

9.2 Present: simple / continuous / perfect

1	am looking	9	is speaking	17	looks
2	Do . . . know	10	does . . . take	18	is ringing
3	have known	11	have . . . worked	19	have . . . liked – have
4	comes	12	have . . . slept		
5	is coming	13	am working	20	has been – is . . . talking
6	has come	14	am going		
7	has collected	15	have had	21	have had – have . . . decided
8	stands	16	am having		

9.3 Present perfect: simple or continuous

1	have . . . loved	4	have . . . known	
2	have been doing / have done	5	has . . . been working / has . . . worked	
3	have done	6	has . . . worked	

7   has been getting
8   Have . . . done
9   Have . . . done

10 Have . . . been doing
11 have been fixing
12 have fixed

9.4 Past simple or past continuous

1   did . . . watch
2   were watching
3   did . . . manage
4   discovered
5   did . . . understand

6   won
7   were winning
8   said
9   was stopping
10 was walking

11 met
12 was looking
13 were going
14 looked
15 saw
16 was snowing

9.5 Past: simple / continuous / perfect

1   had . . . stopped
2   caught
3   was driving
4   was going
5   had telephoned

6   was leaving
7   were waiting
8   saw
9   drove
10 stopped

11 were booking
12 tried
13 told
14 had landed
15 did . . . listen
16 had

9.6 Past perfect: simple or continuous

1   had been having (had had)
2   had had
3   had . . . had
4   had . . . worked

5   had . . . been working (had . . . worked)
6   had watched
7   had . . . watched
8   had been watching (had watched)

10 MODAL VERBS

10.1 Word order

1   You might have told me.
2   He must be feeling terrible.
3   You should not have done that.
4   How many days will you be staying?
5   I will have been here six weeks.
6   She would have helped you.
7   It must have got lost in the post.
8   I would never have known.

10.2 The correct verb form

1   tell
2   do
3   be – working

4   have – had
5   have – done
6   have – been – driving

7   have – had
8   be – arriving
9   be

10.3 Continuous formation

1	be going	5	be having
2	be helping	6	be getting on
3	be leaving	7	be staying
4	be working	8	be arriving

10.4 Perfect simple formation

1	have been	3	have been	5	have helped	7	have been –
2	have done	4	have gone	6	have got		have won

10.5 Perfect continuous formation

1	have been teaching	3	have been having
2	have been sleeping	4	have been playing

10.6 The correct verb formation

1	take	3	have taken	5	have heard
2	be taking	4	come	6	have walked – have given – be freezing

11 OTHER VERB CONSTRUCTIONS

11.1 Word order

1	You needn't finish it.	5	I had better talk to him.
2	You ought to be there by now.	6	I am going to get a new job.
3	I have got to work late.	7	Did you have to wear a uniform?
4	I was not able to finish it.	8	We never used to work so hard.

11.2 The correct verb form

1	to have	5	been – to walk	9	used – to be – to do
2	had – be	6	used – to go	10	to have – got – to working
3	got – to do	7	used – to staying	11	need – go
4	need – to spend	8	am – to have – to talk		

11.3 Need

1	needn't	3	need	5	needed to	7	needn't
2	need to	4	don't need (won't need)	6	needed	8	didn't need to

11.4 Have to

1	have to	3	don't have to	5	doesn't have to	7	has . . . had to
2	has to	4	had to – had to	6	didn't have to		

11.5 Be going to

1 I'm going to be	5 I was going to tell
2 I'm not going to tell	6 We were just going to leave
3 it's going to be	7 Are you going to change
4 are you going to buy	8 I wasn't going to go

11.6 Used to

1 used to live	4 didn't use to work	7 used to getting up
2 used to play	5 didn't use to get up	8 used to get up
3 never used to be	6 used to getting up	

11.7 The correct verb formation

1 ought to be	4 had better clean	7 be able to come
2 ought to have left	5 needn't have given	8 was able to start
3 used to work	6 had better be getting	

12 MODAL MEANING AND USE

12.1 Can or could

1 can	3 could	5 can	7 could
2 could	4 could	6 can	8 can

12.2 May or might

1 might   2 may   3 might   4 may

12.3 Can / could / might / be able to

1 Can / Could	4 can / are able to	7 was able to / could
2 could / might	5 couldn't / wasn't able to	8 might
3 can	6 can't / couldn't	

12.4 Will / shall / would

1 shall	4 will	7 will	10 would
2 will	5 would	8 will	11 will
3 would	6 would	9 would	12 would

12.5 Must or should

1 should	3 must	5 should	7 should
2 must	4 should	6 must	8 must

12.6 Probability and possibility

1	shouldn't	3	must	5	can't	7	might
2	might	4	should / must	6	might	8	must

12.7 Obligation – present and future time

1 should
2 have (got) to / need to – don't have to
3 needn't / don't need to / don't have to
4 must / should
5 needn't / don't need to / don't have to
6 must
7 have (got) to
8 don't need to – should
9 needn't
10 must

12.8 Obligation – past time

1 had to see
2 didn't have to see
3 had to go
4 needn't have gone
5 should have been
6 needn't have worried
7 shouldn't have been
8 didn't need to

12.9 **Will** or **be going to**

1	won't	4	will	7	will	
2	will	5	Are . . . going to	8	am going to	
3	isn't going to	6	am going to			

13 PASSIVE

13.1 Understanding

1	We don't know.	3	No.
2	Yes.	4	Yes.

13.2 Word order

1 Has a decision been taken yet?
2 Now the truth can be told.
3 They had not been told about the meeting.
4 I was told by my grandfather.
5 Where will the 1996 Olympic Games be held?
6 He was arrested by the police.
7 He has been given the Nobel Prize.
8 This machine has to be seen to be believed.

13.3 The correct form of **be**

1	was	3	be	5	were	7	are
2	been	4	being	6	be	8	be

13.4 The correct verb formation

1	are advised	**3**	have been made	**5**	to be bought	**7**	has been delayed
2	be left	**4**	was produced	**6**	be provided	**8**	had been shot

13.5 Active to passive

1 How is that spelt, please?
2 Finally, he was recognised by an old school friend.
3 He was expected to win the race (by everybody).
4 I'm sorry, but it just can't be done.
5 My grandmother was killed by the earthquake.
6 That old hotel has been closed down.
7 The top of the building can be seen from thirty kilometres away.
8 She must have been told about it.
9 Has he been seen in the last few days?
10 Why wasn't I told about this before?
11 Don't worry! We won't be seen from here.
12 I arrived to find that the game had been stopped because of the weather.

13.6 Active or passive

1 He is well known by everybody.
2 (We can use passive but it is better to use active here.)
3 (We cannot use passive here.)
4 (We can use passive but it is better to use active here.)
5 My car has been bought by a tall dark stranger.
6 (We cannot use passive here.)
7 Help! I've been bitten on the leg (by an insect).
8 (We cannot use passive here.)
9 ... They should have been replaced ages ago.
10 (We cannot use passive here.)
11 We are sorry to inform you that you have not been selected for the job.
12 (We can use passive but it is better to use active here.)
13 This book is published by Penguin.
14 (We can use passive but it is better to use active here.)
15 ... I've been given a scholarship by the British Council.
16 (We cannot use passive here.)

14 NOUNS AND NOUN PHRASES

14.1 Counting and plurals

1	villages	**9**	crashes	**17**	policemen
2	(pieces) of homework	**10**	information	**18**	(pieces) of advice
3	people	**11**	leaves	**19**	(metres) of material
4	(pieces) of news	**12**	pollution	**20**	(glasses) of water
5	pairs of pyjamas	**13**	families	**21**	months – teeth
6	children	**14**	fish	**22**	(pieces) of furniture –
7	(kilos) of rice	**15**	(pieces) of toast		desks
8	(pieces) of luggage	**16**	(pieces) of paper		

14.2 Proper nouns

Margaret Thatcher grew up in Grantham, a small town in Lincolnshire in the north of England. She became a Member of Parliament in the 1950s and became leader of the Conservative Party in 1977. She became Prime Minister of the United Kingdom of Great Britain and Northern Ireland after the general election of 1979. Like all elections in Britain, it was held on a Thursday. She is the first woman leader of a large industrialised nation in Europe. Like all the prime ministers before her, she went to live in 10 Downing Street. Downing Street is in London, close to the Houses of Parliament.

14.3 Verbal nouns

1	travelling	6	smoking	11	smoking	16	blowing
2	smoking	7	putting	12	arguing	17	being
3	to smoke	8	talking	13	to look	18	punching
4	smoking	9	to look	14	talking	19	to stop
5	to remind	10	apologising	15	sitting	20	doing

14.4 The correct noun form

1	women	5	beliefs	9	child	13	music
2	women's	6	men	10	children's	14	shopping
3	woman's	7	people	11	children	15	clothes
4	woman	8	family	12	Maria's	16	office

14.5 Genitive noun phrases

1 It's a children's playground.
2 London is the capital of England.
3 He is the mayor of London.
4 It's a five-door car.
5 I met a friend of mine.
6 It's the town hospital.
7 She's the Director's secretary.
8 He was the people's choice.
9 It's the university car park.
10 It's tomorrow's world.
11 They are my cousin's friends.
12 She is my cousins' daughter.
13 It's a language school.
14 It's a phonecard.
15 It's a cardphone.
16 It's a coffee machine.
17 He's Maria's fiancé.
18 It's a baker's shop.
19 It's a clothes shop.
20 It's a car battery.

15 PRONOUNS

15.1 Personal pronouns

1	my	7	us	13	them	19	it
2	mine	8	it	14	It	20	our
3	You	9	hers	15	They	21	they
4	They	10	his	16	theirs	22	it
5	him	11	it	17	You – yourself	23	myself
6	yourself	12	herself	18	us		

15.2 Relative pronouns

1 who   3 where   5 which   7 where – who
2 whose   4 (blank) 6 (blank)

15.3 **That** as a relative pronoun

1 that   3 where   5 that   7 where – that
2 whose   4 that   6 (blank)

15.4 Personal pronouns or relative pronouns

1 who / that   3 who / that   5 who / that   7 Their
2 They   4 who / that   6 who / that   8 whose

15.5 Third person pronouns

1 one   4 it   7 them   10 one
2 it   5 ones   8 one   11 them – one
3 one   6 They   9 them

16 DETERMINERS: THE ARTICLES

16.1 **A / an / some / any**

1 a   3 a   5 a   7 a   9 some   11 any
2 an   4 any   6 any   8 an   10 some   12 some

16.2 **Some / any** with **one, body, thing** and **where**

1 something   4 anywhere   7 something
2 anyone / anybody   5 anything   8 Someone / Somebody
3 somewhere   6 anyone / anybody

16.3 **A / an / some / any** alone or in compounds

1 anything   5 anywhere
2 any   6 a
3 Someone / Somebody   7 anything
4 some   8 somewhere

16.4 **A / an / some / any** or **the**

1 the – a   6 a   11 A
2 the – some   7 the – the 12 the
3 the – a   8 a   13 the
4 the – any   9 The   14 a
5 the – any   10 the

16.5 A / an / some / any or zero

1 a	**3** (blank)	**5** some	**7** (blank) – any
2 (blank)	**4** (blank)	**6** (blank)	

16.6 The or zero

1 (blank)	**13** (blank)	**25** (blank)
2 the – the	**14** (blank)	**26** the
3 (blank) – (blank)	**15** (blank)	**27** (blank)
4 (blank) – the	**16** (blank)	**28** The
5 the – (blank)	**17** (blank)	**29** (blank)
6 (blank)	**18** the	**30** the
7 (blank)	**19** (blank)	**31** (blank)
8 the	**20** (blank)	**32** (blank)
9 (blank)	**21** the	**33** (blank)
10 (blank)	**22** the	**34** (blank)
11 the	**23** the	**35** (blank)
12 The	**24** (blank)	**36** the
		37 the

16.7 The correct article

1 a	**8** a	**15** (blank)	**22** (blank)	**29** The
2 (blank)	**9** (blank)	**16** the	**23** the	**30** the
3 the	**10** the	**17** the	**24** the	**31** a
4 (blank)	**11** The	**18** (blank)	**25** the	**32** the
5 an	**12** the	**19** the	**26** the	**33** the
6 the	**13** the	**20** (blank)	**27** (blank)	**34** some
7 The	**14** The	**21** a	**28** a	**35** (blank)

17 OTHER DETERMINERS

17.1 This / that / these / those

1 this	**4** these	**7** that	**10** that	**13** this
2 those	**5** That	**8** That	**11** this	**14** This
3 that	**6** this	**9** This	**12** This	**15** This – those

17.2 Many / much / a lot (of) / lots (of)

1 much	**5** Many / a lot of / lots of	**9** many	**13** much
2 many	**6** much	**10** much	**14** a lot / lots
3 many	**7** a lot of / lots of	**11** a lot of / lots of	**15** a lot – much
4 much	**8** many	**12** much	

17.3 A few or a little

1 a few	**3** a little	**5** a little	**7** a little
2 a little	**4** a few	**6** a few	**8** A little

17.4 *Of after determiners*

1	of	3	of	5	of	7	of
2	(blank)	4	(blank)	6	(blank)	8	(blank)

17.5 *No / none / some / any alone or in compounds*

1	any	5	Some	9	Nobody	13	nothing – Some
2	no	6	no	10	anybody	14	somebody – anybody
3	none	7	nowhere	11	Somebody		
4	none	8	Some	12	Nowhere		

17.6 *All or every*

1	Everything	3	all	5	Every	7	All
2	All	4	every	6	All	8	Every

17.7 *Every or any alone or in compounds.*

1	anyone	4	any	7	Everywhere	10	everything
2	everyone	5	anyone	8	anywhere	11	anything
3	Every	6	everyone	9	Anything	12	anything

17.8 *Both / either / neither*

1	both	3	neither	5	both	7	either – both
2	either	4	either	6	Neither		

17.9 *A / an or one*

1	a	3	a	5	a	7	One
2	one	4	a – a	6	one		

18 SENTENCES AND CLAUSES

18.1 *Word order*

1 Is that the car that caused the accident?
2 Do you think he is telling the truth?
3 Let me ask you a question.
4 I know you prefer your coffee black.
5 I am surprised that you lent him money.
6 I don't know if he knows about it yet.
7 They think there is a thief in their office.
8 I'm sure that that is the man that hit me.

18.2 Relative clauses

1 A greengrocer is a person who / that sells fruit and vegetables.
2 That's the supermarket that / which stays open late.
3 I know a place where beautiful wild flowers grow.
4 That's the man (who) I know over there.
5 He is a pop star whose songs are popular all over the world.
6 The policeman (who) I saw was very helpful.
7 The Lapps are people who live in the far north of Scandinavia.
8 I met the family who / that live next door.
9 The family (who) I met live next door.
10 The policeman (who) I saw was taking notes.
11 I saw a policeman (who was) taking notes.
12 Pollution is a problem which / that people worry about.
13 The big problem which / that people worry about is pollution.
14 The only book (which) I know on this subject is written by J. R. Smith.
15 I would like to live in a place where there is no pollution.
16 It was a photograph which / that someone had found on the street.

18.3 Empty subjects

1 It is forbidden to talk to the driver.
2 There are four bookshops in this town.
3 In December 1988, there was a terrible earthquake in Armenia.
4 It is horrible to lose your keys.
5 There are several reasons why the building fell down.
6 There were only five cars left.
7 There was a strange man at the window.
8 It was Maria at the window.
9 It is time for us to go.
10 There is a lot for us to do today.
11 It is five years since I last saw her.
12 There is still a lot that I don't know.

18.4 The correct verb

1	suggest	3	let	5	stop	7	left
2	advise	4	allow	6	wonder	8	forgotten

18.5 The correct verb form

1	were	3	to see	5	stay	7	to meet
2	standing	4	installed	6	to help	8	to leave

18.6 Noun phrase + verb

1 We found him doing his homework.
2 I want those windows washed.
3 I want you to look after her.
4 The teacher kept us working until half past six.
5 We had the carpet cleaned.

6 I saw the robbers shoot him.
7 They left him lying by the roadside.
8 Why don't you let them go.

18.7 Clauses with **that** / **if** / **whether** + *question words*

1 The teacher told us (that) we had passed.
2 The teacher told us (that) we had passed.
3 The teacher has told us that we have passed.
4 I was certain (that) he was going to jump.
5 We'd better find out if the plane has landed.
6 I can't understand why he likes that programme so much.
7 I asked him if he had seen Maria.
8 I just didn't know whether to tell them about it.
9 The teacher wanted to know why we were late.
10 He said he would be home by ten but it's half past already!
11 John agrees (that) it's a stupid idea.
12 He asked me what I did for a living.

18.8 The correct meaning

1 We wish you a very happy birthday.
2 He called me a liar.
3 That hat makes you look silly.
4 She taught the boys geography last year.
5 Their laughter made him angry.
6 I think you should try another doctor.
7 I'm sure there is another way to do this.
8 Could you lend me £20?

19 ADJECTIVES, ADVERBS AND COMPARISON

19.1 Word order

1 He can run very fast.
2 He is a very fast runner.
3 There were ten big green bottles on the shelf.
4 He is our new science teacher.
5 Our new TV is very nice.
6 The English teacher seems friendly.
7 It was a beautiful cassette recorder.
8 The new football stadium was expensive.
9 They've built a new Olympic swimming pool.
10 This is my new Amstrad word processor.
11 It is much too expensive for us.
12 It isn't big enough for us to fit in.
13 There was just enough food.
14 The food was not tasty enough.

15 I never miss the London Film Festival.
16 The British shipbuilding industry is dying.
17 It used to be the largest in the world.
18 Her homework is always completely correct.
19 It was more difficult than we expected.
20 We have just met a really nice person.

19.2 The correct form

1	careful	6	hardly	11	early	16	far
2	carefully	7	harder	12	earlier	17	nearer
3	careful	8	hardest	13	earliest	18	farther / further
4	hard	9	simply	14	better	19	most – best
5	hard	10	probably	15	faster		

19.3 Almost / hardly / just / really

1	really	4	really	7	hardly	10	hardly
2	just	5	almost	8	almost	11	really
3	really / just	6	hardly	9	almost	12	just

19.4 Too / enough / very

1	very	4	too	7	very	10	too
2	enough	5	enough	8	too	11	very
3	very	6	enough	9	enough	12	very

19.5 Forms for comparison

1	more comfortable	5	slowest	9	hottest
2	safer	6	bigger	10	most unpleasant
3	faster	7	more uncomfortable	11	easier
4	most ridiculous	8	larger	12	greener

19.6 Phrases for comparison

1	little – than	4	(blank) – than	7	by – the
2	as	5	as – as – of	8	as – as
3	the – in	6	(blank) – than		

19.7 Sentences of comparison

1 Ireland is (a) better (team) than England.
2 England is not as good (a team) as Ireland.
3 The USA is (a) worse (team) than Canada.
4 Ireland is (a) much better (team) than the USA.
5 The USA is not nearly as good (a team) as Ireland.
6 John has got a little less (money) than Maria.
7 John has got far less (money) than Peter. / . . . much less . . .
8 Maria has got a little more (money) than John.

9 Peter has got much more (money) than Maria.
10 Peter is much richer than the other two.
11 Peter is by far the richest of the three.
12 Athens is much cheaper than London or Brussels.
13 London is a little cheaper than Brussels.
14 The cost of living in Brussels is a little higher than in London.
15 Brussels is much more expensive than Athens.
16 You don't need nearly as much (money) to live in Athens as you do in Brussels. / ... as you need in Brussels.

19.8 The correct meaning

1 She teaches English extremely well.
2 This is the fastest car on earth.
3 That was the most exciting match I've ever seen.
4 These books are too big for this shelf.
5 This shelf is not big enough for these books.
6 The Spanish team is not quite as fast as the Portuguese.
7 She almost didn't have time to finish.
8 This car costs less than any other car (you can get).
9 He gets paid more than anybody else in the world of sport.
10 John is (just) as intelligent as Maria.
11 It doesn't rain nearly as much in Somalia as it does in Kenya.
12 She only just passed the exam.

20 TALKING ABOUT TIME

20.1 Word order

1 I never usually forget things.
2 We often go out in the evening.
3 This factory works 24 hours a day.
4 Don't you ever take a break?
5 Always look carefully before crossing the road.
6 I won't ever forget the day school finished.
7 There is a market here three times a year.
8 I worked in a shop after the factory closed down. / After the factory closed down, I worked in a shop.

20.2 Ago or before

| 1 | ago | 3 | before | 5 | ago | 7 | ago |
| 2 | before | 4 | ago | 6 | before | 8 | ago |

20.3 Late

| 1 | later | 3 | late | 5 | lately | 7 | late |
| 2 | late | 4 | lately | 6 | later | 8 | late |

20.4 Already / still / just / yet

1	yet	**4**	just	**7**	still
2	yet	**5**	already	**8**	still
3	just	**6**	yet	**9**	just

10 already – still
11 already

20.5 In / on / at

1	At	**4**	At	**7**	at	**10**	in
2	In	**5**	On	**8**	At	**11**	at
3	in	**6**	at	**9**	on	**12**	on – in

13 on – at – in

20.6 By or until

1	until	**3**	by	**5**	until – by
2	by	**4**	until	**6**	until – by

20.7 Since / for / in

1	since	**3**	for	**5**	since	**7**	in	**9**	for – in
2	for	**4**	in	**6**	since	**8**	for	**10**	in – for

20.8 The correct word

1	for	**4**	Then	**7**	then	**10**	never
2	from	**5**	usually	**8**	Once	**11**	often
3	to	**6**	by	**9**	every	**12**	twice

20.9 The correct meaning

1   They haven't fixed the car yet.
2   I get up early every morning.
3   I never get up late in the morning.
4   She always remembers my birthday.
5   The shop was open from eight to half past eleven.
6   He didn't arrive until half past three.
7   I don't usually watch TV.
8   Every Tuesday and Thursday, I go to evening classes.
9   We haven't met since January last year.
10   We went to the concert after we went to the café.
11   We went to the café and then we went to the concert.
12   I've lived here ever since I moved from the city.

21 BASIC PREPOSITIONS OF PLACE

21.1 Geographical position

1	in	4	on	7	at	10	in
2	in	5	to	8	in	11	on
3	in	6	in	9	off	12	on

21.2 At or in

1	at	3	in	5	at	7	at
2	at	4	at	6	in	8	in

21.3 in or on

1	in	4	on	7	in	10	in
2	on	5	in	8	on	11	in – on
3	in	6	on	9	on		

21.4 At / in / on

1	in	5	in	9	on	13	in
2	at	6	on	10	in	14	on
3	on	7	in	11	at	15	in
4	at	8	at	12	on	16	in

22 PREPOSITIONS OF PLACE AND MOVEMENT

22.1 In / into / to

1	to	4	to	7	into	10	into
2	into	5	into	8	in	11	in
3	in	6	in	9	in	12	to

22.2 To / at / from

1	to	4	at	7	from	10	(blank)
2	(blank)	5	(blank)	8	at	11	from – to
3	to	6	from	9	(blank)		

22.3 Some prepositions of movement

1	past	5	into	9	through	13	through
2	through	6	across	10	through	14	past
3	through	7	across	11	into	15	into
4	towards	8	round	12	across	16	towards

22.4 Off / out / out of

1	off	**5**	off	**9**	off	**13**	off
2	out of	**6**	out of	**10**	out	**14**	out of
3	out	**7**	out of	**11**	out of	**15**	out – off
4	out	**8**	off	**12**	off		

22.5 Over / above / up / on top of

1	over	**3**	above	**5**	over	**7**	on top of
2	on top of	**4**	up	**6**	above	**8**	over

22.6 Under / below / down / underneath

1 below **2** under **3** down **4** underneath

23 HOW AND WHY

23.1 Word order

1 We went straight to bed because we were tired.
2 We were tired so we went straight to bed.
3 Because we were tired, we went straight to bed.
4 We were so tired that we went straight to bed.
5 This chair is made of plastic.
6 There was a traffic jam and as a result I was late.
7 He spoke quietly so that nobody would hear him.
8 It was playing so quietly that nobody could hear it.
9 I moved the bookshelf so that there was enough room for the TV.
10 We left early because there would be lots of people there.
11 There is no public transport. As a result, most people have cars.
12 I took a taxi so that I'd arrive early.
13 We got good seats because we left early.
14 We left early so we got good seats.
15 I took an umbrella as I expected it to rain.
16 I expected it to rain so I took an umbrella.

23.2 By / for / to / with

1	with	**5**	for	**9**	to	**13**	by
2	by	**6**	by	**10**	for	**14**	to
3	by	**7**	With	**11**	with	**15**	for
4	for	**8**	By	**12**	by	**16**	with

23.3 Because / so / as a result

1	because	**4**	because	**7**	because	**10**	because
2	so	**5**	As a result	**8**	because	**11**	so
3	so	**6**	so	**9**	so	**12**	As a result

23.4 *So or such*

1	such	3	such	5	so	7	such
2	so	4	such	6	so	8	so

23.5 *So / so that / so . . . that*

1 They were very tall so it was easy to find them.
2 He is so tall that he has to wear special clothes.
3 They were wearing strange clothes so (that) it was easy to find them.
4 They put on strange clothes so that it would be easy to find them.
5 She did so well in her exam that she won first prize.
6 The lecture was so boring that I fell asleep.
7 I made a list so that I wouldn't forget anything.
8 I had forgotten something so I had to go home and get it.

23.6 *Connecting ideas*

1	by	4	to	7	Because	10	such
2	because	5	so	8	so that	11	that
3	so	6	by	9	As a result	12	for

23.7 *The correct meaning*

1 The plane was too expensive for us to take.
2 I can't afford cigarettes because they are too expensive now.
3 Because cigarettes are very expensive now, I can't afford them.
4 Cigarettes are so expensive now that I can't afford them.
5 So that I wouldn't forget it, I put it next to the door.
6 Because I didn't want to forget it, I put it next to the door.
7 The exam was so difficult that nobody passed it.
8 The wind was blowing so strongly that I couldn't hear what he said.
9 It was such a strong wind I couldn't hear what he said.
10 We left early so (that) we could / would get good seats.
11 We can make sure it arrives by sending it express.
12 You can't make an omelette without breaking eggs.

24 *SIMILAR AND OPPOSITE IDEAS*

24.1 *And or or*

1	and	3	and	5	or	7	and
2	or	4	and / or	6	and	8	or

24.2 *And / also / both / so / too / as well*

1	and	3	too / as well
2	also	4	and – so

138

5	and – both	8	and – so
6	also	9	Both – and
7	and – and – as well / too	10	and

24.3 *Either / or / neither / nor*

1	either	4	Neither – nor
2	or	5	neither
3	either – or	6	either

24.4 *Although / but / however / on the other hand*

1	but	3	but	5	Although	7	On the other hand
2	Although	4	However	6	On the other hand	8	However

24.5 *And / both / but / either / or*

1	either – or	4	and – both	6	but
2	but	5	but	7	and
3	but			8	or

24.6 *The correct meaning*

1 Both John and Maria should be home by now.
2 John should be home by now and so should Maria.
3 He is neither fast nor careful.
4 I would rather watch the match on TV.
5 The weather is fine but it is very cold.
6 We can see either the film or the football match.
7 Maria has lost her bag and so has John. / . . . John has too / as well
8 Maria can't find her bag and neither can John. / . . . nor can John

25 *SEQUENCE AND CONDITIONS*

25.1 *Understanding sequence*

1	having lunch	5	same time
2	having lunch	6	same time
3	John arriving	7	having lunch
4	having lunch	8	John arriving

25.2 *When / while / and*

1	and	3	When	5	and	7	when
2	While	4	while	6	when / and	8	While / When

25.3 *After or after that*

1	After	2	after	3	After that	4	after that

25.4 Showing sequence clearly

1 I was watching TV when the doorbell rang.
2 While I was watching TV, the doorbell rang.
3 The doorbell rang while I was watching TV.
4 I turned off the TV when the doorbell rang.
5 When the doorbell rang, I turned off the TV.
6 Before I opened the door, I turned off the TV.
7 I turned off the TV before I opened the door. / . . . and then I opened . . .
8 I opened the door after I turned off the TV.

25.5 Understanding conditions

1 Possibly. 3 No. 5 No. 7 Yes.
2 Possibly. 4 No. 6 No. 8 Yes.

25.6 The correct verb formation

1 rains	5 didn't rain	9 opened
2 was not raining	6 hasn't left	10 have
3 stops	7 hadn't left	11 had
4 hadn't rained	8 open	12 have / had

25.7 Making conditional sentences

(Possible answers)
1 If I hadn't spent all my money on clothes, I could go on holiday.
2 If I didn't spend all my money on cigarettes, I could go on holiday.
3 If I hadn't passed the exam, I wouldn't be at university now.
4 If I see Maria there, I can tell her the news.

25.8 The correct meaning

1 If you don't get out, I'll punch you on the nose.
2 Unless John has forgotten his key, we can get in. / . . . has lost . . .
3 Turn the power off before you correct the fault.
4 Before I leave, I'll have another cup of coffee.
5 I'll leave after I've had another cup of coffee.
6 If John comes to the party, we can arrange it then.
7 If John had come to the party, we could have arranged it then.
8 If I had a terrible toothache (like you), I would see the dentist.
9 Would you mind if I brought my baby with me?·
10 Is it alright if I bring my baby with me?
11 If I could remember his name, I would introduce you to him.
12 I would have said hello if I had seen you there. / . . . but I didn't see . . .

EXTRA EXERCISES

1 Apostrophe s ('s)

1	is	3	genitive	5	has	7	genitive	9	has
2	has	4	is	6	is	8	is	10	genitive – is – has

2 Apostrophe d ('d)

1	would	3	had	5	would – had
2	would	4	would	6	had – would

3 More tag questions

1	mustn't you?	5	would you?	9	do you?	13	hadn't they?
2	won't you?	6	wouldn't you?	10	isn't he?	14	were they?
3	can they?	7	should she?	11	haven't we?	15	did he?
4	won't we?	8	could you?	12	hadn't we?	16	didn't he?

4 Used to / past simple / past continuous

1	did . . . understand	5	used to stay
2	did . . . use to understand	6	was staying
3	used to understand	7	used not to be / didn't use to be
4	stayed	8	used to talk

5 Verb formations for future time

1	will have / am going to have	7	is going to be / will be
2	am going to have	8	am seeing / am going to see / will see
3	is having / has	9	is coming / is going to come
4	Are . . . doing	10	will talk
5	is coming / is going to come	11	will know
6	is hoping / hopes	12	are going / are going to go

6 Active or passive with the verb be

1	trying	5	helped	9	inviting
2	surprised	6	repairing	10	invited
3	surprising	7	repaired	11	growing
4	helping	8	invited	12	grown

7 Singular or plural

1	comes	6	are	11	has	16	hates
2	are	7	is	12	have	17	hate
3	is	8	is	13	has	18	have
4	are	9	is	14	have	19	are
5	comes	10	is	15	likes	20	knows

8 There / their / they're

1	They're	4	They're	7	they're		10	They're – their
2	Their	5	Their	8	their			
3	There	6	there	9	There – there			

9 Where / were / we're

1	Where	4	Where – were	7	we're
2	were	5	where – were	8	where – we're
3	We're	6	where	9	were

10 Telling the time

1 twenty past eight in the morning
2 twenty past nine in the morning
3 twenty past two in the afternoon
4 a quarter past eleven in the morning
5 half past four in the afternoon
6 a quarter to eleven in the morning
7 eleven o'clock in the morning
8 two minutes past eleven in the morning
9 a quarter past two in the morning / . . . at night
10 ten to seven in the morning
11 five to ten in the evening / . . . at night
12 twenty-five to eight in the evening

11 Dates

1 the first of January, nineteen eighty-nine / New Year's Day . . .
2 the second of November, nineteen eighty-seven
3 the fifth of June, nineteen ninety-two
4 the twenty-fifth of December, ten sixty-six / Christmas Day . . .
5 May the first, nineteen seventy-seven
6 the eighth of April, nineteen ninety
7 January the eighteenth, nineteen fifty-two
8 October the twenty-first, nineteen eighty-eight
9 the eleventh of November, nineteen eighteen
10 August the thirty-first, nineteen eighty-eight
11 the seventh of September, nineteen twenty-four
12 the ninth of July, nineteen fifty-one